FROM
PLAN
TO
PLANET

to Lois —
one love,

[signature]
07-03

Life Studies:
The Need
for
Afrikan Minds
and
Institutions

Also By Haki R. Madhubuti

Poetry
Think Black
Black Pride
Don't Cry Scream
We Walk the Way of the New World
Directionscore: Selected and New Poems
Book of Life
Earthquakes and Sunrise Mission
Killing Memory, Seeking Ancestors
Criticism
Dynamite Voices: Black Poets of the 1960's
Anthologies
Say That The River Turns: The Impact of
Gwendolyn Brooks
To Gwen, With Love (co-edited with Pat Brown and
Francis Ward)
Confusion By Any Other Name: Essays Exploring
the Negative Impact of the Blackman's Guide
to Understanding the Black Woman
Essays
Enemies: The Clash of Races
From Plan to Planet, Life Studies: The Need for
Black Minds and Institutions
A Capsule Course in Black Poetry Writing
(co-authored with Gwendolyn Brooks,
Keorapetse Kgositsile and Dudley Randall
Black Men: Obsolete, Single, Dangerous? African
American Families in Transition
Records/Tapes
Rappin and Readin
Rise Vision Coming
(with the Afrikan Liberation Arts Ensemble)
Mandisa
(with the Afrikan Liberation Arts Ensemble)

FROM
PLAN
TO
PLANET

Life Studies:
The Need for
Afrikan Minds and Institutions

By Haki R. Madhubuti

THIRD WORLD PRESS

First Printing, February, 1973
Tenth Printing, February, 1992

All Rights Reserved

Some of these essays have appeared previously in
*Black World, Black Position, Third World, Afrikan
World, Black Books Bulletin* and *Amsterdam News.*

Asante sana to Sister Cheryl Catlin for the cover
design. Asante also to Brother James Ray for the
jacket photograph and to Brother Kofi for photo-
graphs of IPE New Concept Development Center.

ISBN: 0-88378-066-6
LC#:   72-94350

Manufactured in the United States

INTRODUCTION

We must recognize the force of ideas. European ideas translated into the "American Way" and forced on us have to a large degree transformed Black people in the United States into a new people. Yes, we are Afrikans, but more than any of us would like to admit -- we are Afrikans of the West. And to be honest most of our people see themselves as more Western (American) than Afrikan or Black. We Afrikan-Americans (or Afro-Americans) are a nation within a nation. The cultural energy that a people needs to generate and maintain their own ideas, that is, their concept of themselves as well as how they think the world should operate, depends to a large extent on cultural influences -- theirs or somebody else's -- that are operating

Afrikan traditional culture in the United States to a significant degree has been drastically altered (or lost) in the acculturation process. That is, western cultural aggression has been committed against Afrikan people ever since our initial contact with Europeans. In the process of survival (adjustment and submission) we have, indeed, become a **new people**. Euro-Americans have forced their values on us and in our acts of rejection as well as submission we have been transformed into Afrikans of the West; sometimes referred to as Negroes, Niggers, Colored People, darkies or coons...depending upon the political and cultural situations one may find oneself in.

I speak of this because as we re-issue **Plan to Planet** we do so without alteration. This is not to say that none is needed, but other pressures/commitments do not allow me at this time to do major revisions in some of the essays. Therefore the reader must keep in mind the historical context in which much of **Plan to Planet** was written. **Plan to Planet** came out of the sixties and early seventies. However it is mainly a work of the sixties. It speaks to an urgency and to a **way of life** that is still with us. The oppression of Black people in the United States has become more subtle and widespread. In the latter part of the seventies much of the Black "middle class" felt that they had escaped the race "problem" however with the Bakke decision; the death of much of the Affirmative Action programs; the rise of the neo-conservative movement and the New Right; the legalization of the Ku Klux Klan; the energy crisis, and the white flight back to reclaim the cities; many Blacks are beginning to reassess their lives in a racial, cultural and political context.

The call for a new printing of **Plan to Planet** has been phenomenal and one hopes that the ideas within have been actualized at some level by the readers. As you read please keep in mind that much of what is written about in the book has either been put into action or is being attempted. With that experience we have been able to re-evaluate our work and the Black struggle and have published another book of essays which should be read as a complement to **Plan to Planet** -- **Enemies: The Clash of Races** (Third World Press, 1978).

As always I hope that we have left you with something of value. Remember, we are **one people** and that we can do what we **work** to do.

Haki R. Madhubuti
Institute of Positive Education
8/27/79

A sound man by not advancing himself
Stays the further ahead of himself,
By not confirming himself to himself
Sustains himself outside himself;
By never being an end in himself
He endlessly becomes himself.

—LAO TZU

Comments:
by an Afrikan* in America

AFTER MANY YEARS OF POLITICAL AND EDUCATIONAL
activity, kept in perspective by much studying, I've come to the conclusion that our survival lies in our ability to produce a secure, competent, work-oriented, incorruptible generation of black men and
women who will operate out of an Afrikan frame of reference based

*FOUR REASONS FOR USING K IN AFRIKA.
  1. Most vernacular or traditional languages on the continent
spell Afrika with a K; therefore the use of K is germain to us.
  2. Europeans, particularly the Portugese and British, polluted our
languages by substituting C whenever they saw K or heard the K
sound—as in Kongo and Congo, Akkra and Accra, Konakri and
Conakry—and by substituting Q wherever they saw KW. No European language outside of Dutch and German have the hard C sound.
Thus we see the Dutch in Azania calling and spelling themselves
Afrikaaners. We are not certain of the origin of the name Afrika,
but we are sure the name spelled with the C came into use when
Afrikans were dispersed over the world. Therefore the K symbolizes
our coming back together again.
  3. The K symbolizes to us a kind of Lingua Afrikana, coming
into use along with such words and phrases as Habari Gani, Osagyfo,
Uhuru, Asante, together constituting one political language, although
coming from more than one Afrikan language.
  4. As long as Afrikan languages are translated (written) into
English, etc., the European alphabet will be used. This is the problem. The letter K as with the letter C, is part of that alphabet, and
at some point must be totally discontinued and the original name
of Afrika used. The fact that Boers (peasants) in Azania also use
the K, as in Afrikaan (to represent the hard C sound) demonstrates
one of the confinements of the alphabet.

upon a proven black value system that incorporates a sense of Afrikan love and responsibility. I say this not out of a total negation of my generation, or that of my parents, but on a realistic assessment of our situation in this country and in this world. We must produce a generation of Afrikans who are willing to fight at a new and more sophisticated level.

We, along with our parents and their parents, have, consciously and unconsciously, internalized the values and aspirations of our oppressor to the point that we are himself. We have become so soft and dis-oriented in our life style that luxuries (eg: expensive clothes, well-furnished apartment or home, two cars, ten credit cards, vacations every year, three meals a day, three college degrees, etc.) have become needs. We have adopted the value system of the European-Americans to the point that everything in life that is not European- or American-centered is alien to us, and considered unnatural; just notice how black people in the country rebel against being called what we actually are, *Afrikans*. It is not for me at this time to document our strangeness—a close reading of Frantz Fanon, Paulo Freire, E. Franklin Frazier, Albert Memmi, Sterling Plumpp and others have adequately done this. But, the major point is that we've ceased to be a responsible people (this can be seen in the abundance of the two major killers in the black community—drugs and poor education). We have ceased to be responsible to ourselves, to our race, and to our children. And without a sense of responsibility we cannot act responsibly, and freedom, in its fullest sense, requires people that are responsible to themselves first and the world second.

Our sense of priorities has been distorted to the point that many of us do not have the necessary air of urgency about us that is absolutely needed. Our sense of urgency is generally directed toward positioning ourselves in a comfortable slot with all the trimmings, vis-a-vis white America. It is madness, because we don't possess the major criteria for position, status and power, which is to be white. Yet, our wanting and needing to be white is at best a profound comment on the acute state of our sickness.

This book is a result of years of work, study, love and frustration. (Even though the manuscript itself was produced in the last two years, the actual theory and practice have been in effect, at some level or another, for about ten years or more.) The frustration that conscious black men and women undergo in this country is nothing less than extraordinary. The psychological stress and strain that the West puts on us (depending upon our consciousness) is vast, and for us to remain sane and politically active under such weight is a phenomenon of the mind and body.

This book, as indicated by title, is motivated toward the working of and building of Afrikan minds and institutions that will deal systematically and sensibly with the problems of Afrikan people while focusing on national/local struggles in relationship to the world struggle. At the outset I tell you that this work is insufficient—other works will come, by me and by other brothers and sisters better qualified to assess and analyze the need or non-need of Afrikan Institutions. However, we felt that a groundbreaking work from IPE was necessary.

I believe that much of what is written has been written before; much of what is said has been said before. What each generation gets is a re-appearance of information in a style and context that speaks to their needs and wants, that speaks to their particular void. The little knowledge I share with you did not develop out of a vacuum, did not develop in some closet away from the real world. I have had many teachers and that which is positive and responsible about this book is due to their commitment in teaching me and others. Their names are many, but I would like to pay special thanks to the following: The Honorable Marcus Garvey, Osagyfo Kwame Nkrumah, the Honorable Sekou Toure, Mwalimu Julius Nyerere, the Honorable Elijah Muhammad, El Hajj Malik Shabazz, Maulana Karenga, Mao Tse Tung, Ho Chi Minh, Chancellor Williams and Imamu Amiri Baraka. Special thanks is to be given to the staff of the Institute of Positive Education for their encouragement and criticism—without it this book would not exist. I should also point out that my current position as Writer-in-Residence at Howard University has aided me in understanding the unbelievable bureaucracies and insecurities that exist at black colleges. This is not a slick criticism, but the acknowledgment of a reality that took me somewhat by surprise. I give all my love and thanks to all the beautiful Afrikans that *work* and *study* daily to bring about the reality of the unification and empowerment of Afrikan people. Their example has been a major source of inspiration and direction. At this time let me state that whatever is negative and irresponsible about this work I alone stand responsible for and humbly ask your forgiveness and comment.

> Asante sana, (Thank you very much)
> Don L. Lee
> 1 October 1972

Contents

In each of us
An Afrikan mind
will
be the basis for creating anything
Afrikan
nothing Afrikan is created without
an Afrikan mind that is
Creative

The Survival
of Black People:
Is it Possible?
(NEEDED, A NEW SOPHISTICATION)

THERE ARE INSTITUTIONS IN THIS COUNTRY THAT DO nothing but create, study and solve problems. It doesn't matter what the problem is. These institutions tackle everything from "the necessity of nuclear warfare in the 21st century" to "the urbanization of the rural Negro" or better yet "the containment of the Negro in urban centers." These institutions exist at Harvard, M.I.T., the University of Michigan, U.C.L.A., etc. There are also "independent" branches of these institutions such as the Council on Foreign Relations, the Hudson Institute, the Center for the Study of Democratic Institutions and the all powerful RAND Corporation, notoriously known for producing "The Pentagon Papers."

These study groups are generally referred to as "think tanks" and work in conjunction with and in many cases exclusively for the federal government. For example, the Asian Studies Department at the University of Michigan and U.C.L.A., were of critical importance in the briefing of Nixon and his army of coat tails before they ventured into China. These institutions in places like the "Situation Room" at RAND have fought simulated wars for the next fifty years with a projected eye on how to come out on top (they've rewritten Sun Tzu's *The Art of War* and people like Herman Kahn are the new theoreticians—see *On Thermonuclear War* and *Thinking About the Unthinkable.*

We tell you this because it seems to us that two qualities in our struggle are absolutely needed: 1) a new sophistication of struggle and 2) a new automatic association (comradeship) among Afrikan people. We understand that the rebellions of the Sixties were not expected by the "authorities" and the "authorities" were therefore taken by surprise (Detroit was a good example), which is to say that one of the reasons we didn't lose as many lives as one would normally expect is that the white boy didn't know what he was up against. He didn't know if the rebellions were planned or unplanned. This uncertainty hindered his reaction. But, in the 1970's he not only knows what he's up against, but he has built five or six defenses to deal with what ever comes out. This is why we call for a new sophistication in our struggle based on all the available knowledge of modern struggle and warfare that we can get our hands on. This is to say that, with a new sophistication, we not only call the plays but understand the game we are playing.

Our second point is that we must begin to educate our own people like the halls of education in Europe and America educate their own. For example, a Henry Kissinger or McGeorge Bundy did not develop in a vacuum; everything about their lives (mainly at the student-adult level) has been planned and mapped out to near perfection. We can trace Henry Kissinger's public life from Harvard to the Council on Foreign Relations to the Rockefeller Brothers Fund to the Center for International Affairs (Harvard) to the State Department under Nixon. In this we see how Government and the Academic world work together. This is to say he was groomed for his job like blue-bloods groom blue-bloods for inter-marriage. A Kissinger does not develop over night; it takes years of training and personal attention from the trainers.

Where are black men being trained? Mostly on the street corners or in the prisons. Why is it that our brothers do not develop a level of black consciousness on the outside that they develop inside? Why is it that most brothers gain their political awareness inside the prisons after 99 years to life has been slapped on them? Well, mainly because we have failed to build the necessary institutions that educate and re-direct our men. We get sent to prison and *then we think* about our place in the world because there *is nothing else to do.* We discover our blackness in an environment that by definition, rules us powerless to do anything about it other than personally grow while possibly influencing the few bloods we are in contact with in prison.

In our new wisdom it is fundamental that we begin to institutionalize our thoughts and actions and we need institutions for that. Yet, even beyond institutions we need more realistic association between brothers and sisters in the diaspora and Afrika. Afrika must exist for us like Israel exists for the Jews; every Jew realizes that his future, realizes that his raw existence, is dependent upon the continuation and growth of Israel, which doesn't mean that every Jew will migrate to Israel, but every Jew—Zionist or not—will support Israel. Because they understand the necessity for a land base away from their enemies, even if they plan to live among their enemies for tactical and economical reasons.

What we are suggesting is that early Afrikan association be instituted so as to pull us closer together, not only in our various tribes in the U.S.A., but also in the diaspora. We must return to the extended family concept where Brother John on 43rd and Cottage Grove in Chicago is tied by race tradition and direction to Brother Joe and Sister Ann on 79th and King Drive and all are tied to Brother Kwame and Sister Ife on the continent of Afrika. Our relationship as brothers and sisters must become automatic so that we automatically—consciously or unconsciously—work toward the same goals: The unification and enpowerment of Afrika and its people.

We must begin to build toward this end while understanding that white people (Europeans) are the world's chief obstructionists and will invest all available time, money and energies keeping *us* apart. The major thing that the European-American fears is Afrikans coming together. The one thing that will keep them together is *our* coming together. They fear that worse than *anything*.

On the other hand European-Americans (all white people) have always acted in their best interest vis-a-vis *everybody else,* whether they be black, brown, yellow, or red people. An excellent example of this is how the British, Portuguese and American governments through NATO (which includes much of Western Europe) have kept men like Vorster of South Afrika and Smith of Rhodesia in power. The United States in the interest of big business such as Interantional Telephone and Telegraph, Polariod, Hoover Company, the Chrysler Corporation, etc., have worked through the appropriate British subsidiaries who in turn invest in their South Afrikan subsidiaries that maintain the apartheid policies in South Afrika. Openly this government has supplied arms to Portugal. These arms are also produced by private industry in the United States. If these armaments do not find their way into the racist hands directly, they come indirectly through NATO. The effect is the same. White people, automatically, whether they reside in Europe, the United States, Canada, Guinea Bissau, Rhodesia, South Afrika or the West Indies look after each other at the expense of everybody else. This must be understood and if we are wise, a good lesson is there for us.

However, we must not define our selves or our struggle on their evil. We can't build a movement on anti-white man, anti-capitalism or anti-Europe/America. No! We build on pro-black people, pro-Ujamaa (Co-operative Economics), pro-Pan-Afrikanism, thus defining ourselves in the positive and not only giving direction by our definitions, but values—values that would not be evident if we defined in the anti-tradition. Also, by defining in the positive, the negative is defined. If we're for Co-operative Economics we're by definition against anything that is opposed to that.

Finally, we decided to *live for the people, not die for the people.* Everytime we lose a brother or sister we lose a worker, a builder, an energy force for our tomorrow. Regulate your life toward life. Be aware of the Complicated and sophisticated world we face. Don't let us in our naivete and Afrikan emotionalism drive ourselves to the point of no return. A blazing poem or paragraph ain't never stopped a mad white boy with a 357 magnum. Remember, few black people in this country understand the *Art of War* yet, we are always talking warfare. There is a reason for *that* and our enemies are aware of it, too. Watch your words while improving your actions. It is not how well you say *what needs to be done,* but how well you *do it.*

We Are an Afrikan People

SINCE OUR FORCED MIGRATION TO THIS LAND WE'VE been defined by various terms. All have been in some way or another negative, e.g., negroes, niggers, coons, colored people, Afro's, studs, etc. By definition, if one is defined from the negative and assumes said definition, one, in all likelihood, will act and perceive the world in a negative way. By negative we mean: viewing, functioning, learning, growing, defining and identifying the *purpose* of a people by somebody else's *frame of reference* which causes a people to act wholly against its own self interest, at the expense of its own numbers, to satisfy the interest and aspirations of somebody else. Black people's *frame of reference* in America (how we view and operate in this world) has been reversed from that of our Afrikan selves to accepting the frame of reference based upon the value system of Europeans and European-Americans.

The basic contradiction is that we are not white and European, nor are we white and American; therefore, everything we do to mold ourselves into such will ultimately fail because we do not possess the major criterion—that of whiteness. Genetically, all black people's place of origin is Afrika. Our history did not start here and will not end here. Our ties to Afrika are cultural, political, economic and emotional. We were brought here as Afrikans and over a period of 353 years or more we have become negroes, colored people, Afro-

Americans and an assortment of nonentities unmentionable in essays of this type. It should also be noted that wherever we were dropped in the western hemisphere we took on local definition, e.g., West Indian, Guyanese, French-Indian, Afro-European, etc.). However, other ethnic people who exist in these various places maintained their identity and fused their culture into the larger reality. In this country, there was adaptation on both sides; few Europeans have come here and wholly given up their identity for something as nebulous as Americanhood. The Irish remain Irish, the Italians remain Italian, the Polish remain Polish, the Jews remain Jewish and so forth. Ethnics from other parts of the world such as Asia also retain their cultural characteristics and national identity. The Chinese remain Chinese, the Japanese remain Japanese and they understand that even if they call themselves Chinese-Americans or Japanese-Americans that, in the *final* definition imposed upon us all by white Anglo-Saxon Protestants, they are first and foremost Chinese and Japanese people. Witness the horror-spectacle during European 20th Century War no. 2 (known as World War II) wherein all the "Americans" of Japanese descent (about 110,000 people) were detained in concentration camps while Germans and Italians, whom this country was fighting too, remained their American selves outside the camps.

People define themselves in accordance with their own values using tradition and reason that is uniquely theirs. Chinese came from China and are Chinese, Japanese from Japan call themselves Japanese, Europeans from Europe fit their identities to the appropriate sub-nations of Europe, but in a European context; and Afrikans from Afrika should call themselves Afrikan regardless of their differences. These definitions reinforce each group's own sense of purpose and historical necessity. By associating oneself with a particular culture, a particular history and a particular land base, one's sense of identity and direction can be clarified in terms of a people's own best interest, vis-a-vis their enemies and the world. Thus, their interest can be understood in a more realistic way, i.e., the Jews know that they are Jews and they know that they have to fight 365 days a year wherever they are in the world, to remain Jews and to keep Israel as a Jewish homeland. That is reality.

But, for Black people in this country, what is a "negro?" Did we name ourselves "negro?" Where is "negroland?" Who is an Afro? Is there an "Afro" culture? Is there an "Afro" history? If so, give me a book of history on the "Afro." You'd probably have to go to a barber shop or beauty college because an Afro is the way you wear your hair. There are no people named Afro's; there is no land named Afro-land. White boys and girls are wearing their hair in an Afro style. Does that make them "Afros" too? To call ourselves Afro cnly haphazardly, in an around-about way suggests that we have some connection with Afrika. Finally, we're not "colored people." Yes, we are people of color, but a *distinctive* color which is *black* (in all its beautiful variations) and the original and current land of black people is Afrika, not Europe or America.

However, our confusion is not unusual. The minority ethnic of most nations have always tried to assimilate into the dominant community, which, under proper circumstances, is natural. The first half of the 19th century saw the Jewish community seeking such assimilation wherever they resided in Europe. That is, a great many Jews sought to become French, German, Prussian, British, etc., rather than Jews, so that their identity as Jews was realistically threatened by extinction. This is to say that Jews, during their assimilating period, did not consider themselves *a people* (a Jewish People). Yes, they considered themselves a community, a neighborhood, maybe a minority religious group, but during assimilation many were baptized Christians, and many others practiced the religion of the "higher" culture of Europe, the arts and sciences. According to Walter Laqueur's *A History of Zionism,* "German Jews . . . did not believe in the existence of a Jewish people; they had no real understanding of the nature of anti-semitism; there was no real Jewish life—it was all stuffy, unreal, divorced from the people, lacking warmth, gaiety, colour, and intimacy." It was not until the European pogroms became widespread and systematic that the Jews began to consider themselves a specific people. They were forced to for their own survival.

Our problem, too, is one of identification. We *do not consider ourselves a people*—an Afrikan people. We identify ourselves as black Christians, black Muslims, negro NAACP'ers, black businessmen, black teachers, Afro-doctors, colored musicians, or black this-and-that. What we've done, in most cases, is take the European definition and put black in front of it and still work within a European Frame of Reference. However, if we define ourselves as a people, as an Afrikan people, and set up the necessary mechanisms and institutions that will re-educate people to such, we will then begin to act and not re-act in the best interests of Afrika and Afrikan people, which is what *all* other ethnic groups do naturally. Will it take Afrikan pogroms to move us into this position?

We are Afrikan people in America, defining ourselves from the positive (Afrikan) toward the negative (American). As our consciousness becomes tuned to the reality of our situation in this world, we will begin to see the commonality of the problems Afrikans face where ever we are and that to see ourselves as Americans in the final analysis is to side with our enemies. Our major problem is that we are defining our existence out of a European context, thus we are starting from the negative. If our definition is based upon the opposite of or reaction to whiteness we still will be coming from the negative. That is, if white Europeans *didn't exist,* according to logic, we wouldn't exist because our definition is based on their existence, on their reality and not our own. Once we create our own frame of reference, we'll begin to see that to be an Afrikan is not only strength and beauty, but is a necessary prerequisite for bringing together all the various tribes—whether we are located in South America, the Caribbean, Asia, Europe or North America. We are an Afrikan people who must begin to act and think in concert with the Afrikan world if we are serious about the survival of Afrikan people worldwide.

Re-taking the Takeable

to create or recreate an Afrikan mind
in a predominantly european setting   demands
serious work & has no wonder drug.
to recreate Afrikans is not a 12 week course
at UCLA with thanksgiving and christmas off
there will be no coffee breaks or 3 week vacations in the bahamas
we prepare to retake our minds   like
our enemies prepare for war.

we're trying to recapture
the substance & the future of ourselves
trying to recapture
the direction of our young.
it took a war to take them from us   and
it will take nothing less than a war
to return the minds of Afrikans
to their rightful owners.

The Need
for an Afrikan Education

OUR POSITION ON BLACK EDUCATION IS VERY CLEAR
and simple. Either a people prepare their youth to be responsible
and responsive to their *own needs* as a people or somebody else will
teach them to be responsible and responsive to somebody else's needs
at the expense and detriment of themselves and their people. Mwalimu Julius Nyerere has stated that the "purpose of (education) is to
transmit from one generation to the next the accumulated wisdom
and knowledge of the society, and to prepare the young people for
their future membership of the society and their active participation
in its maintenance or development." The most important asset a
people has is its young. Without children there is no continuation,
there is no future. You cannot build a black nation or a world with
just one generation; we need generations. We need a youth that can
complete that which we start, a youth that can challenge the future
we're bound for. We need an offspring that is skilled in the necessary
areas of world building.

In the 1970's it is not a luxury to be able to read and write, it is
a requirement; it is not a privilege to be able to compute the speed
of light, measure the distance between two points, or understand the
intricacies of tele-electronics, it's a necessity. It is not just for Europeans to be able to navigate the universe, explore the oceans, or in-

vestigate the beauty of the brain. The 21st century is upon us and will demand of our children unknown *effort,* unknown *discipline,* unknown *dedication*—will demand skills and expertise unthought of by the average man of 1972—will instill in our children the necessary skills and values that will motivate them to serve Afrika and Afrikan people.

Our minds, the lifestyle that we have, and the vision that we possess have all been shaped by our education. The reason we find it difficult living and working with each other (black people) is that we've been taught from birth to work against ourselves. We, in our actions and outlook on life, in many cases, are more American than the white boys, or, as we call them at IPE, the Europeans (all people of European extraction, whether they exist in Canada, USA, Israel, South Afrika, or the Caribbean). Historians like Toynbee have always regarded the United States as an extension of European civilization.

We feel that only Europeans can teach Europeans to be European (that is, to act and function in the interest of Europe and its subnations); only Asians can teach Asians the Asian way of life, and only Afrikans can guide Afrikans toward a lifestyle that is consistent with the survival of Afrikan people, and will enable bloods in Afrika and the diaspora to advance, create, and build *as a people.* The reference to *as a people* as opposed to *as individuals* is to focus primarily on the ability of the collective body (two heads are better than one, three better than two, and so on) rather than on the arms and legs of one man. To intrust the minds of our young to Europeans is equivalent to blowing their brains out ourselves, for all we will receive in return are brothers and sisters who are confused about their *identity, purpose,* and *direction,* and in effect have been tortured to a slow death.

European people, in their bid to control and manipulate the world, recognized the imperativeness of education and used it as a survival weapon for themselves. It is not an accident of nature that most references pertaining to goodness and purity are white and most references denoting evil and impurity are black. *The powerful re-order the world in their image and create a new frame of reference for everybody.* The European advancements in science and technology are not due to a natural superiority over other people, but, as Imamu Amiri Baraka points out, is due to "their ability to physically and mentally hold everybody else back while at the same time on may levels build, invent, and create for their own interest at the expense of others." If, we, as a people, are so busy trying to be white, trying to love white, trying to act and live white in a world that will only accept us if we are *actually* white—we should be in the position that we're in. To want to be white in a world where the majority of the people are of color is in itself a sickness. To have internalized the values and aspirations of the oppressor to such a degree again emphasizes the need of a people to educate its own, if it wishes to keep its own. To turn our children over to others is to run the risk of losing them forever.

The major ideology that has shaped our actions for the last five or six hundred years (which is only a drop in the ocean in terms of history) has been the Jewish-Christian Ethic—which is no more than the fusion of Jewish and Christian history, culture, politics, education, religion, technology, and values. The concept of the individual over and beyond that of the collective group is utmost in the Judaic-Christian Ethic. Obviously, the most damaging value pushed to the "colonized" people of the world *other than to be white is best* is that of the importance of the "individual" man over that of the collective body. That is, individual achievement is encouraged over that of group achievement (UJIMA—collective work and responsibility) even at the expense of the group's accomplishment. Of course, the end results are that the individual, at some point, will begin to think that he or she is not only more important than the collective group, but the *Nation* itself. The competitive and aggressive aspects of the European man are stressed over the co-operative and complimentary nature of the Afrikan man. Unity (UMOJA) becomes a hollow word, at best, because the entire system of politics, education, commerce, and culture, is Europeanized toward anti-humanism. The accomplishment of the singular is given preference over that of the plural. History, tells that very few feats are accomplished alone. You can't build and staff a school alone; you can't teach people their history, culture, values by yourself; you can't run a hospital alone, you need brothers and sisters at every level—orderlies, doctors, nurses, psychiatrists. No one man can run a hospital. You can't talk up on some UMOJA (unity) or UJIMA (collective work and responsibility). You have to live and practice it—and it's best to start early because the most critical period of a child's learning is between the ages of 3 and 6. And of course the best teacher is consistent and concrete example. Yet, what we do with our children during those critical years is a cultural crime of the highest. No other people would send children to the enemy for education. *If our children, in their later years are to be responsible to us, we, in their youth, have to be responsible in educating them.* Nobody can instill black values except black people. Our ability to conceptualize and act for our future depends upon who's been feeding us our concepts.

The Chinese on the West Coast almost started a war when the city told them that their children would have to be bused out of the community. The Irish in Chicago would rather close down their schools than have their children educated with blacks or by blacks. Jews, because of their education, don't have to be asked in later life "Will you work for your people?"; that concept is quietly accepted from the earliest years and looked upon by the Jew as a duty and a privilege. Two of our greatest killers in the black community are drugs and education. Yet, you can't deal with the first without realistically dealing with the second. Drugs are accepted and used because of a lack of *identity, purpose,* and *direction* which are in keeping with the goals of Afrikan people worldwide.

The time for talking is over; we know what has to be done. Anyway, the way brothers *rap* today—if rap was money, we'd all be rich. The only problem any over-abundance of talking can solve is that of silence. We need doers rather than sayers. We need, as Mwalimu Julius Nyerere suggests, an educational system built by blacks "that fosters the social goals of living together, and working together, for the common good. It has to prepare our young people to play a dynamic and constructive part in the development of a society in which all members share fairly in the good or bad fortune of the group, and in which progress is measured in terms of human well-being, rather than prestige buildings, cars, or other such things, whether privately or publicly owned. Our education must, therefore, inculcate a sense of commitment to the total (Afrikan) community, and help the pupils to accept the values appropriate to our kind of future, not those appropriate to our colonial past." To continue to send our children to strangers for the cultivation of their minds will make them strangers to their own people. You don't see Jews sending their children to Arabs for their education. The Chinese don't send their children to Russians for an education. Why is it that we, Afrikans in America, trust our children to the care of any and everybody, and expect them back, black, and ready to work for their people? It won't happen, and we won't be here to write about it if we don't, today, change the course of the wind.

Where Are
the Black Educators
Who Are Educated Blackly?

A LITTLE KNOWLEDGE MIS-USED IS DANGEROUS; A great amount of knowledge *not* used properly is criminal. It has become increasingly clear that "black educators" are not going to provide the direction needed to save the minds and creative spirit of our children. As long as they opt for positions and status in European institutions, realistic movement will never come. Their egos and individual insecurity have not allowed them to view the problem beyond that which they can personally benefit for themselves, i.e., positions as professors, department heads, model cities directors, postal supervisors, and assistant-assistant department heads, etc. The majority of the so-called professional class of blacks who, by definition, have led the black community are Europe-educated; that is from twelve to fourteen years their training has taught them to act, move, think, talk, relate as European-Americans (commonly referred to as white people). This orientation cannot be wiped out in one session of black enlightment, cannot be eliminated by reading a few black books. The psychological damage that has been done to us in this country may be irreparable. However, we must have the attitude that since we already, according to Maulana, possess the *first* criteria

35

for blackness—our *color*, it is possible with *time* and an institution-alized re-education of ourselves to acquire the other two criteria, those of *culture* and *consciousness*. With our culture we begin to identify with each other, to understand our purpose in life and are thus potentially able to give our children *direction*.

We live in a country where less than 6% of the world's population uses over 60% of the world's natural resources. This is achieved with a deliberate and calculated mis-use of the majority of the world's people. But stating this we are immediately put on the defensive and accused of spreading racist propaganda. However, the facts tell us that the power of this country is mainly fed from the outside. The United States is like an octopus with its tentacles in most of the "developing" nations. This country is virtually bare of natural resources, so that it is absolutely necessary to maintain its hold over others, to tie up or control the natural resources of the world, if possible. Hoyt W. Fuller has pointed out that black people (and other ethnic groups), "just don't know how the *world* works." What he is saying is that the *world* is not just Chicago, is not Washington, D.C., is not New York, is not Paris, is not Moscow, is not Peking. The *world* is those points plus smaller and larger points throughout the world. What about Afrika? What about South America? What about other parts of Asia? Do those areas function in this world? We couldn't prove their existence from the literature, magazines, newspapers or news programs read and viewed here. But, if we black people begin to understand our relationship to the larger world, hopefully it will enable us to understand our association to other brothers and sisters who occupy this same *world* we think belongs to somebody else. We have to begin to understand that problems in Chicago are not just problems shared by blacks in Chicago. We, in order to deal with the world, have to understand who runs it, and that the powerlessness of Afrikans in South Afrika is no less than that of Afrikans in the West—just less sophisticated. We need to understand that it is not a trick of fate that keeps black people on the bottom all over the world, wherever we are. Let's look at the world a little closer.

Who is dealing in death daily in Viet Nam and has just about literally destroyed a country by dropping more bombs on that small nation than have ever been dropped in all the past wars of all nations? European-Americans! European-Americans who know that this country could *never* defeat the Vietnamese people on *land* so they destroy the land, destroy the *food* source in order to weaken the people. Who does this? Americans and Europeans! *Who* is forcing our brothers in South Afrika to work in *their* diamond mines for less than 35c a day—and have brainwashed people like Roy Wilkins and Eartha Kitt to visit and voice that *their* solution is *dialog* and *jobs* (you can't talk a hurricane into stopping its destruction). The Afrikans don't want *jobs;* they want *their land back.* Who is behind this again? European-Americans—with the help of a few negroes! Who is controlling other parts of Afrika physically and economically —for example in Zimbabwe where less than 300,000 Europeans rule over 5 million Afrikans; the Afrikans virtually have no say-so over their own life style. Yet, can you imagine 300,000 Afrikans in London ruling 5 million Englishmen? Who keeps these Europeans in power? European-Americans! Portugal could not continue its colonialist fight in Guinea-Bissau without the aid of the United States (through NATO), Gulf Oil and the catholic church. Portugal could not exist without European-American finance. Who has moved to control all the industry and land in South America? ITT controls over 70% of the communications network and the Great Fruit Company owns the majority of the vegetable and fruit produce coming from our brothers there. Again, European-Americans. Who in the black community here controls the destiny of blacks, controls the institutions, the life giving and life saving institutions that give *identity, purpose* and *direction?* Again European-Americans. And, finally, after they get tired of messing over the world, they escape into the Caribbean—the islands—which has become their playground and has turned many sisters into lightweight prostitutes and brothers into junior hustlers of the Shaft, Super Fly type. *Who,* again? The European-Americans. Brothers and sisters, this is not racism or fantasy on *our* part. These are the facts. The job of the 21st century black educator is to have internalized these facts and to be about the business of creating a mechanism, a structure, institutions to systematically dissiminate these and other facts into the community they claim they are a part of, to be about the task of getting these facts and others to the streets they say they represent, to impart this new life saving knowledge to the people they say they *love*. When will the black educators and other professionals become accountable to the black community? The last twelve to sixteen years of liberal education has made them into liberals, unsure of the space they occupy, if they occupy any. They're sure not invisible; we see right through them and we know, in the final countdown they'll be sprinting that last mile to get back in. It may be too late.

Sister Johari M. Amini, in the IPE pamphlet *An Afrikan Frame of Reference* has said

> . . . Europeans definitely do not accept an Afrikan's definitions of anything for themselves. But not only do they not accept Afrikan authorities as being able to make legitimate definitions for them, they extend this even further for their own welfare: Europeans do not even accept Afrikan authorities as being able to make legitimate definitions for *Afrikans,* the reason being that Afrikan definitions based on Afrikan referents would not only contradict and oppose European definitions, but would conflict with European needs, interests, goals and backgrounds, and begin to eliminate them.

A good example for us to look at in the Seventies is China. Nixon's ability to go to China in 1972 is significant; yet even more significant is the reception he received. When Nixon stepped off Airforce 1 in China, he didn't see multitudes of Chinese people in a frenzy waving American flags talking about "take me back with you!" No, he saw that the army was there to greet him. When Nixon and his party traveled into the interior, we didn't observe Chinese people running up to them quoting John Q. Adams, George Washington or Marx and Lenin. They quoted Mao, Confucious and Chou En Lai. Why is this?

For the last twenty to twenty-four years, the Chinese people have been about, with the systematic use of *Chinese culture,* re-creating a Chinese mind. This took twenty years, not twenty weeks. For the last twenty or so years, they closed their borders to outside influences and programatically began to bring back the Chinese personality, the Chinese language, the Chinese music, dance and literature, to bring back the total Chinese way of life, and after a generation they can allow something as unusual as a Nixon to visit without fear of losing one Chinese to the American way. The Chinese had won the major battle, that for the minds of their people.

The Brazilian educator Paulo Freire has said that

> The oppressed, who have adapted to the structure domination in which they are immersed, and have become resigned to it, are inhibited from waging the struggle for freedom so long as they feel incapable of running the risks it requires. Moreover, their struggle for freedom threatens not only the oppressor, but also their own oppressed comrades who are fearful of still greater repression. . . . They discover that without freedom they cannot exist authentically. Yet, although they desire authentic existence, they fear it. They are at one and the same time themselves and the oppressor whose consciousness they have internalized.

This brings back the black saying, "He outwhites the white boy." Which is where the majority of us are. What Freire is saying is that we've become so americanized internally and externally that a fight against our oppressor is also a fight against ourselves and before we can effectively deal with the world's enemy, we must conquer the enemy within. Logic tells us that the longer you have lived with the internal enemy, the longer it will take to rid yourself of it. If we understand this, at least we know that we need an institutionalized structure to help save our children. This is where inedependent black institutions come in: independent (void of outside control and influence), Black (in color, culture and consciousness), institution (a structured program aimed at correcting a deficiency, giving concrete alternatives).

In the book *Planning an Independent Black Education Institution*, prepared by the Independent Black Education Institutions Division of the Council on Education and Black Students of the Congress of African People, edited by Brother Frank J. Satterwhite, some basic realities of our present educational system are pointed out:

1. More than 99 percent of our children are presently educated in white-controlled institutions. Further, we can expect this situation to prevail for some time to come. It is given then that *at present* we

do not have the human and material resources to educate our own black children.

2. White-controlled educational institutions are destroying the minds of 99 per cent of our children by building within them a spirit of European nationalism.

3. It is inherently contradictory to attempt to implement a Black Curriculum, a Pan-African Curriculum, in a white-controlled setting —the setting must be Black-controlled.

4. We are about the business of providing quality education, an African alternative for African children, youth and adults.

5. The development of the national Pan-African School System is a long-range program, our present responsibility being to train a cadre of New African Men and Women prepared to lend their skills to the development of new social institutions.

6. *We will survive . . . we will conquer . . . we will educate our own . . .* WITH OR WITHOUT MONEY!

7. We cannot afford the luxury of failing to utilize the skills of all African people that can assist us in the development of our Pan-African School System.

8. Our institutions and our communities must be *one* with maximum involvement of students, parents, teachers, administrators and community residents.

9. *Our youth can learn and will learn if we provide them with an educational environment for learning.*

10. If our educational programs are good, the Black community will legitimize us; if they are not, the Black community has an obligation to alter our problems or destroy them.

11. It is probable that even with maximum planning, our institutions will develop on a "trial and error" basis, that we will learn by doing and as we do, we will minimize the errors.

In all fairness to black people in education, the reason we don't have many black "educators" is that few have been *trained for that purpose*. Few have been given a Black Value System to work with. Yet, we have to start somewhere and the most logical place other than the *home* itself is the other greatest influence on young minds—the schools and the streets (to deal with the streets would take another essay). However, only Black educators can fulfill the educational needs of black people; to expect our needs to be met by our natural enemies is circus talk at best. The Black educator must realize that *it is unrealistic to talk about change if you are not moving to control the instruments of change in your community*. Genocide comes in many forms, but the most subtle and damaging is the genocide of the mind and at this point in time we can't plead ignorance.

Afrikan institutions are necessary
so as to help deliver Afrikan man into
a higher state of peoplehood
into a higher state of completeness.
Afrikan institutions are not to misuse the world
but to compliment its positive aspects.
Afrikan institutions are to help in the completion
of the world in its purest form
by instilling in our people identity, purpose and direction.
If we see value in this
we see value in Afrika and the institutions of
Afrika

Institutions:
From Plan to Planet

IN THIS WORLD, WHICH IS FAST APPROACHING THE 21ST century, the Afrikan's major problem is that we don't realize, internationally, that we all have the same problem, which is, in part, our inability to define for ourselves, out of our own context, the struggle in which we're engaged. This struggle, if properly defined by using history and logic as a criterion, would then be put on an international scale, accenting local struggles as a base for bringing the various tribes together under the Afrikan umbrella. Hopefully, by analyzing our problem locally, nationally, and internationally once and for all, without fear, we'll recognize that the world's enemy, not just the Afrikan's enemy, is the European: whether in England, Germany, U.S.A., Portugal, etc. It is no accident that wherever Black People reside in this world, whether in North America, the Caribbean, Afrika, or Europe, where Europeans occupy the same area we're below the first step: economically, politically, educationally, socially, as well as culturally. And, whenever we begin to fight against obvious mis-appropriations of power, whether with mass actions or through the use of "legal" means (as if a butterfly has rights in a spider's web), we are the ones defined as "the racist" and put on the defensive, as if we raped Afrika of ourselves and transplanted ourselves by the millions to other parts of the world to build a "civiliza-

43

tion" for somebody else. Even today (1972) some Black People believe we swam over here or walked on water, or possibly were the first people to fly. Because to face the facts would in essence require us to face ourselves, to confront our powerlessness, to actually question the right to call ourselves Black men and women, because few of us act in accordance with traditional Afrikan manhood and womanhood.

People occupy space. Whether you control the space you occupy depends in part on 1) consciousness, 2) commitment, 3) action, and in some cases, geography. Some of the main reasons the European countries are able to function so well are: their ability to communicate with each other; their ability to define their problem and organize around it; their ability to produce essential goods and services for their people (at the expense of other people), and their ability to distribute such goods and services while stabilizing their culture and society by building life-giving and life-saving institutions such as schools, hospitals, places to worship, etc., which are based on a common value system that instills in their people European *identity, purpose* and *direction.* And this European value system functions in this world because of 1) *consciousness,* 2) *commitment,* and 3) *actions.*

If you ask the average blood what his ideology is, you'll get such answers as: I don't know what the word means; christian; democratic; republican. Possibly, since *Blackness* is *in,* the blood may say that his ideology is *Blackness,* but if you ask him to define Blackness beyond color, you are bound to be disappointed and/or confused with the answer. So, from the outset we see that basic to our problem is the lack of well-defined directives that can provide us with a working ideology embodying the strengths and weaknesses of our people. Even a brother saying he's Black does not necessarily make him so. The basics of Blackness as Maulana points out are *color, culture,* and *consciousness,* and you can't have Blackness in its totality one without the other. It would be like a car without wheels, a body without a nervous system. You need it all to function properly. To question the brother further as to his race, you might receive everything from, I don't have one, I'm universal, or negro, colored, black, or Afro (which is actually the way you wear your hair), or Afro-American,

Afrikan-American (to say American denotes that you enjoy all the rights and privileges of other Americans) ending, possibly, with "an Afrikan in America." Of course, all this does is add to the confusion, but it is important to point out that such diversity of thought in part explains our diversity of non-action. It is a wonder we made it into to Seventies.

So, fundamentally we understand that most Afrikans in America have become ,after four hundred years of training, "european-Americans" in thought, action, mannerisms, outlook, beliefs, and functional values; as Fanon says—"Black Skins, White Masks." The only reason the physical chains were taken off the first place is that the more sophisticated chains were transferred to our minds and, as you should know, if you control the mind you got the body.

In the 1970's the question that is elementary to our predicament is, can we *create* or *re-create* an Afrikan (or Black) mind in a *predominantly European-American setting?* This is critical. One cannot expect change unless one creates a climate for change. One cannot expect a sincere revolutionary movement of thirty-five million Afrikans outside of Afrika unless we create an Afrikan mind that dictates such movement. No European can create an Afrikan mind. Only an Afrikan can do that. Yet, Afrikans cannot be created out of a vacuum. We need structure. Before you can institutionalize *thoughts* and *actions,* you need institutions and as we say at IPE*, institutions are built around a plan of action and we need to act in concert in a working plan in order to take the planet. You cannot re-order one mind without a plan; you cannot take a block without a plan; you cannot re-shape a school system without a plan; and to nationalize, organize, and mobilize a people you need—a plan. You need institutions that are based upon sound and practical reality, based upon a sound ideology. And, our plan is just that, a working set of directives based upon a sound ideology. And, our ideology is just that, a working set of directives based upon an historical and futuristic assessment of our situation using Afrikan tradition and logic. That is why we say we're Pan-Afrikanists, Black Nationalists, and Afrikan Socialists (UJAMAA); all three areas are connecting

---

*Institute of Positive Education; Chicago, Illinois

and embody knowledge of the present and past, presenting a workable plan for tomorrow for all Afrikans wherever they are. To say we are Pan-Afrikanists is not visionary thinking or theorizing. We believe in one Afrika and the oneness of Afrikan people. As Black Nationalists we believe we must nationalize our thoughts and actions, must establish a national-international Black thought—international Black movement—can a Black in Zimbabwe think and act in concert with a Black on the West side of Chicago? Can the blood in the Caribbean feel the weight of crackers breeding their corruption among us as we feel it in New York City? As Afrikan Socialists, we must go back to the original Afrikan communalism—the basis of all humane governmental systems, the willingness to share and work together, UJAMAA (cooperative economics) and UJIMA (collective work and responsibility). In the states, we call this system, this new body of thought and directives—*Kawaida* ("that which is customary, or traditionally adhered to by black people"). Kawaida, with its Nguzo Saba—or Black Value System—defines for us in the simplest and clearest of terms the directives we must take humanely and scientifically, take for our survival as a people. The Nguzo Saba, the Black Value System, as originated by Maulana Karenga and reactivated and actioned to near perfection by Imamu Amiri Baraka of the Committee for Unified NewArk is: UMOJA (Unity), KUJI-CHAGULIA (Self-Determination), UJIMA (Collective Work and Responsibility), UJAMAA (Co-operative Economics), NIA (Purpose), KUUMBA (Creativity) and IMANI (Faith). This system for Afrikans here should be the basis for everything that we do and is the dominant guide for IPE and Third World Press in Chicago. And, as Imamu says, with these 7 principles "we can move the dead"; they are simple in what they say, but total in that they evoke all the levels of meaning associated with philosophical systems. The 7 principles are "10 commandments" yet more profound to us—US because they are pre- and post-10 commandments at the same time."

Nobody takes bloods seriously because we don't take ourselves seriously. When we begin to re-order life in our image for our future, when we stop acting dead and take control of the vital life-giving and life-saving institutions in our community, then and only then will we be taken seriously by our brothers and the world-runners.

We should never say "to die for the people." We should always be about living for the people. A people are not renewed or redeemed through the sacrifice of martyrs; in many cases martyrs are, in the final analysis, very selfish men who have failed to build a movement (institution) void of their egos, have failed to build a movement around a solid ideological base that relates and fulfills the needs of the people. However, in many cases in the country, luxuries have become needs; for example, in 1972, if the blood had to choose between a cadillac and ideology, the hog would win every time. We are crisis-oriented and only recognize death when it comes swift and unexpected—with a bullet or bomb. Yet, the most permanent death is that of the mind. We can build a defense against a bullet or a bomb, but it is difficult to regain the mind once it has been captured. That is why Afrikan institutions must become the life-cycle of the Afrikan man and woman from conception to the day we join our ancestors. As Brother Sterling Plumpp has said: "If you know what we want people to become, then you can specify what they should experience from birth to adolescence and they will become it. But to do this one must control institutions and Black People don't control institutions. For if Black People controlled the education of black children, then the whole question of culture would not be discussed solely in terms of philosophy, but it would be practiced from day-to-day and adjustments could be made to fit different circumstances." And, the three criteria for culture as defined by Maulana are *awareness, acceptance* and *practice,* which cannot happen unless you control the internal and external mechanisms that instill culture. Because to instill in our brothers and sisters the three ends of culture, those of *identity, purpose,* and *direction,* takes a structure, a plan, takes institutions to enforce and regulate the plan. This cannot be done by an outside force—only bees make honey, just as Europeans make Europeans. You can't get an egg from a gorilla. If we ourselves are not doing it, that means somebody else is doing it for us. In New York, the Jews don't send their children into the Black community to be educated: that is to say, a Jew knows he's a Jew; in New Jersey, the Italians don't send their children into the Black community to study Black music; Italians remain Italians, while our Leontyne Price sings opera; in Chicago, the Irish don't send their children into the Black community for anything. Yet we, without batting an eye, whisk our children off to anywhere and everybody and expect the children to remain their black selves under the Jews, Italians, Irish, the what-have-you. No wonder by the time they reach 18 or 19 they are so confused and don't know what they are; they've become international niggers without *identity, purpose,* or *direction.* We must understand that our children are our major natural resource and to allow others to teach them their values, to allow the enemy to instill their purpose and direction in our children is not only a cultural *crime* of the highest, but will aid in the destruction of a people quicker than the most advanced form of 21st century technology.

The basis of Blackness is *color, culture,* and *consciousness.* The basis of our survival as a people is in understanding, consciously and unconsciously, that the Afrikans' struggle is a common one, that we cannot function as a unit unless we are thinking and acting as a unit. In our community, real change will come about only if we have committed people who are oriented toward positive communal action. Our motto at IPE is KUFANZA KAZI (to Work), KUSOMA (to Study), KUUMBA (to Create), and KUJENGA (to Build) — you can't build anything without these principles, working overtime six and seven days a week, sixteen to eighteen hours a day—remember we're still playing "catch-up-and-capture" rather than "pass-and-develop"; that will come in time, but we must recognize reality as it is in order to shape reality as we want it to be. We close by saying if we can't produce a generation of Afrikans, maybe if we Kazi (Work) we can produce a generation of Blacks concerned about Afrika. The race cannot stand for anything less—the lives of our children are at stake. The decision is ours, and if we love Black people it's an easy one. Which will we take, the cadillac or our future.

Communications:
The Language of Control

A NATION'S ABILITY TO COMMUNICATE WITH ITS PEO-
ple is of major importance in the education (the teaching of culture and values), organization, mobilization and general directions
of a nation's people. The effectiveness of the communications between men and leaders (spiritual and political) and men and institutions (or vice versa) depends, in part, upon the sophistication
of the medium chosen to telegraph such communications and the
ability of the people to receive and understand that which is being
transmitted. Effective communication (i.e., knowledge which
leads to action) also depends upon the medium used for transmission,
radio as opposed to newspapers or both; depends upon the people's
ability to comprehend that which is being communicated; that is,
is there a common language, does basic literacy exist among the
people (being able to read and write and understand the language
being used—in the case of a nation)?

The language you speak is just about synonymous with the
culture you practice. Those who speak English will undoubtedly
act English. It can also be assured that the welfare and well-being
of England and its holdings is very important to English speaking
people. The Chinese people (in mainland China) who are ac-
knowledged Marxist/Leninists do not have Russian as a national

49

language; they speak and act Chinese and the ideology that they use is translated into Chinese and re-ordered to fit the Chinese way of life. This is important because the Chinese language (structure and content) is a sustaining foundation of Chinese culture and nationhood. How else could the culture of the Chinese people have existed for thousands of years (especially with Europeans occupying this same earth)? The unity (Umoja) of a country depends in part upon its literacy and the ability of *all* the people in a given situation to understand and concretely communicate with each other. A people in possession of a common language using that language at its highest, in accordance with the direction dictated by its *culture,* can develop and expand to unknown dimensions.

Another factor in relationship to language is that when one uses a particular language he not only speaks and communicates with it, but also feels, experiences and acts—consciously or unconsciously—in accordance with the cultural, spiritual and political context of it. An Afrikan born and raised in the United States speaking American English will undoubtedly, at some level or another, act more "American" than "Afrikan." His behavior pattern will be more "American" than "Afrikan" even if he consistently tries to be "Afrikan," because to be "Afrikan" requires more than color and desire. It requires a complete re-education, re-orientation as an Afrikan man or woman which will include language, culture, religion, history, politics, etc. This is not an over-night process, and demands of its proponents a great deal of planning and concrete examples, e.g., Afrikans doing what is Afrikan, i.e., in the best interest of Afrika. This is why *Kawaida* ("that which is customary, or traditionally adhered to, by black people") which stresses Afrikan language and the NGUZO SABA (A Black Value System) are so necessary. The use of traditional Afrikan language (we suggest Swahili) puts us back in touch with ourselves and with each other and the NGUZO SABA gives us a basic guide and value system to work from. Traditional language and the NGUZO SABA provide us with, as Maulana has said, "identity, purpose and direction." After all, you very seldom see a Frenchman who can't speak French and is not for France, or a Russian who can't speak Russian and is not for the Soviet Union. The reason Swahili was chosen over other Afrikan languages is that it is in keeping with the second principle of the NGUZO SABA, KUJICHAGULIA, that of Self-Determination—to define, name and speak for ourselves, instead of being defined, named and spoken for by others. Also, as an Afrikan language it is non-tribal, thus avoiding the trap of identifying with one aspect of Afrikan people rather than the whole. Finally, Swahili (in syntax and structure) is collective in concept and practice, thus aiding in the realization of the third and fourth principles of the NGUZO SABA, UJIMA, Collective Work and Responsibility, and UJAMAA, Cooperative Economics. Swahili with its collective nuances rather than individualistic directive, stresses the importance of the co-operative nature of man over the individualistic. Individualism in the 20th century has been one of the major deterrents in keeping the Afrikan in the 19th century. Language is crucial in the mental and physical liberation of a people. The use of our own language in communicating with each other would not only free the mind but put something on it. Language gives direction—positive and negative—because in the final analysis, the question is who is teaching you what, and how is he teaching you. This is what counts!

Let me say again that Swahili was chosen over other Afrikan languages because it is a living example of what we're trying to accomplish, e.g., see Julius Nyerere's *Ujamma*. Swahili is the national language of Tanzania and much of East and Central Afrika are aware of it. Its usage does not invalidate other Afrikan languages and if there is an Afrikan language more suitable for our purpose, by all means, let's rush to it.

One of my students pointed out that the universal language we needed to learn was that of mathematics, technology and science. One can easily agree with that, except those disciplines are not learned in a vacuum divorced from a national language. The Russians teach calculus in Russian, the Chinese teach technology in Chinese and the French teach science in French. There may be a pure mathematical language, but I'm sure it is supplemented or complemented by a "national" language. Why can't that language be an Afrikan language. Why can't the books be translated or written in an Afrikan language? This needs to be done in order for us to circulate the proper values into the study of the sciences. Science is value-oriented just as culture is; science without values is just a duplication of the Europeans—we don't need that!

We're not so naive as to believe that Afrikans here are going to adopt another language—most of us just can make it with English (that should tell us something), but we *must* at a realistic level begin to incorporate Afrikan ideas into our thought and lifestyle and that in itself requires the study of Afrikan language. Also, to be bi-lingual helps explode the myth among blacks and others that we're unable to learn a second language. To consistently use the enemy's languages while consciously undermining him at the same time will continue to take exceptional brothers and sisters. And, as you know, English destroys more brothers and sisters than it saves. We must not forget that we're not just dealing with the way a people talk or communicate, but *how* they're taught to *think*. It is not enough to say "Afrika for Afrikans," you have to be mentally and physically prepared to develop a lifestyle or way of life that is consistently Afrikan as defined by Afrikans in accordance with a workable Afrikan value system and 21st century technology and science. But that has to be communicated to black people by black people who believe it, too, because in the 1970's to say "Afrika for Afrikans" ultimately means to physically *take* Afrika and to *take* Afrika demands a new sophistication that must be rooted in our ability to move, act, think, communicate and fight as a unified *unit* of Afrikans. And Unity, UMOJA, the first Principle of the Black Value System, which is to strive and maintain Unity on seven levels (self, family, community, neighborhood, nation, race and world) is basic to our advance as a body. Swahili as a language brings us together rather than divides us, is a language that emphasizes UMOJA and other necessary values such as NIA (Purpose), KUUMBA (Creativity), and IMANI (Faith), values that are absolutely necessary in developing a nation of Afrikan people here in North America. The English language *is* necessary, but only to the point that we're able to use it to undermine our enemies. When it ceases to do that, we must cease to advertise its so-called universality by using it as efficiently as we do. Undoubtedly, for Nigeria to adopt English as its official language has done more damage to the Nigerian's Afrikan Personality than good. And it will get worse. Another example is the Jews of Germany in 1869 who had become more German than the Germans; "through the medium of language they had accepted German culture, and through culture the German spirit." Yet, all that German culture and language didn't save them seventy years later when Hitler came to power. The English language is for Englishmen. For example, when the Alegrians put the French out of Algeria, they didn't maintain French as a national language, even though most of the people spoke it, but went back to Arabic so as to recapture that which was fundamentally Arabic and Islamic. Language is basic to style or system of life, yet, keep in mind that we must use and develop any tool that we can in our continuous struggle and for me to suggest that black communicators be more conscious of the language that they mis-use is only to underscore the importance of language as a .weapon. Communicators, whether in electronics, arts, written words, music, black ritual or thru tin cans must move beyond being just the "bearer" of the word to that of translator/ interpreter of the Afrikan world, while incorporating "identity, purpose and direction" within each image they re-create. Images control our lives. The abundant use of white sugar, cigarettes, alcohol, cadillacs, comic books, hardware "art" and English should adequately make my point, because we're certainly a people without black "identity, purpose and direction." We are moving to control the image rather than let the image control us and the language of communications as it is used to help liberate our people *must* be consistent in our music, art, fiction, non-fiction, poetry, drama, etc., but above all, must display its effectiveness in the area of the spoken word.

The New Pimps/
or it's Hip to be Black:
the Failure of Black Studies

OUR PROBLEM IS NOT THAT WE DON'T REALIZE WE
have a problem: our problem is that we don't realize we all have the
same problem. The formulation of black or Afrikan-American
studies at today's white colleges and universities is only one of the
super-mistakes made in the Sixties. The future failure of Afrikan-
American studies has been predicted and should not be seen as
accidental by any means.

   The fact of the matter is that you cannot build without a foundation and foundations are not established unless you have sound,
serious and committed people. *Sound:* in the profoundest sense,
knowledgeable in one's field of study and not threatened by staff,
faculty members and others, secure to the point where one's ego
can be subordinated so as not to be harmful to the wishes and aims
of the organization. *Serious:* understanding priorities, willing to
prepare and work to accomplish said priorities. *Committed:* to the
point of a new lifestyle, to the point of new values, ideals and
goals; committed indeed to work that could be considered dangerous,
dangerous in the sense that you'll be challenging the images which
control the world. And when we say the world, we don't just mean

some higher institutions of learning, or New York City, Chicago or Paris the Sorbonne or Cambridge, etc. We mean the world-runners—the white boy!

DOOMED TO FAILURE:

During the latter part of the Sixties, just about every college where a sizeable number of black students existed (sixteen or more), a push for black or Afrikan-American studies was initiated. The problem, other than inadequate planning and lack of foresight, was that we did not have enough competent people to fill all the positions opening up all over the United States. Everybody and their mommas were talking black studies and studying blackness as though it were something new, and it *was* to most of those who were doing all the talking—so new that they actually believed what they were doing was right, necessary.

To quickly put this in a proper context, blackness and Afrikan studies are nothing new. They are new if you've never been exposed. That was the problem; few if any of the proponents of black studies had ever been exposed to any serious study of the black world and its inhabitants. What we had coming in to lead and teach were five year masters, just out of school yesterday (European studies, Humanities, French or Physical Education, etc.) who hadn't heard of blackness and didn't want any part of it until it was *safe,* profitable. But to add oil to fire, we had brothers and sisters who for the last five to eight years were being trained as European-Americans and to come to blackness in many cases was something uncertain, queer and quite alien. They couldn't handle it. They were psychological misfits who could not adjust fast enough and therefore couldn't possibly give any type of positive direction because they didn't have any themselves. If you've been an imitation white boy for the last twenty-six years out of a twenty-six year life span, how could you become black overnight? Not only was there a problem of inadequate and inexperienced personnel, there was never really a serious commitment made by white universities. They all played the wait-and-see game, only giving and taking when it was absolutely necessary. As black students demanded everything from soul food to black dorms, the universities were coolly planning five to ten years ahead. They had the main ingredients for disruption on their side: money and power.

Money emerged as a major obstacle. Yes, money, but not real money and only money in the sense that it was money to those who didn't understand the uses of money and what *real money* is. Here were black brothers and sisters who had been in school for the last six to eight years and in all likelihood had come from poor black families. And if you ain't never had nothing, being confronted with a salary ranging from thirteen thousand to twenty thousand will make most black people say yes, regardless of qualifications—and the main qualification was that the participants be black (in color only) because there were few people around who even had the competence to judge prospective staff and faculty members.

But that's only part of it. We must not forget that our new black staff members, directors and assistant directors were trained to be European-American and that upon receiving salaries equal to their counterparts, they immediately sought a new level of living—a level consistent with thirteen to twenty thousand dollars. So, in effect, we witness the making of a *new* bourgeoisie, a new elite. Instead of cadillacs and houses, we get Mercedes and condominiums. Instead of loud dressing, street talk and the old hustle, we get academic dress, a cool rap with shades of blackness and a black hustle—in other words we get the new pimps, educated pimps.

If salaries were not problem enough, brothers not understanding administrative budgeting and the economics of running a program found out very soon that the funds allotted for the program fell very short. Soon after many of the programs were initiated, because of the ideological differences, small power plays erupted in the departments. There were problems concerning who was going to lead. Were they going to be *Black Nationalists, Pan-Afrikanists, Third Worldists, Marxist-Leninists:* were they going to be community oriented or not, scholarly or not scholarly? Many brothers not being secure in their own manhood failed to understand the basics of the whole movement: first and foremost we're black men and women and the conditions under which we function will dictate and formulate our ideology—which is to say that few of the participants in the early Afrikan-American studies programs really understood the black community and even fewer had an historical perspective to work from. Everybody was in the dark except the white boy. He knew exactly what was happening and what was going to happen. After all, the Jews had been "authorities" on us long before we were "authorities" on ourselves.

They walked the danger course and carried young minds with them. The only identity they had was of themselves as individuals, and reflections of European-Americans. They did what they were *supposed to do,* they did what they were *taught to do.* Now since they've acquired a few possessions and something to *lose,* they become careful and worried about their jobs. Insecure from the beginning because of not being properly prepared, we begin to see that the various staff and faculty members were not able to work and function together as an organization or unit. Not only were they insecure as teachers and scholars, but as black men and women as well. It all came home when they were challenged to produce by the uninhibited and unsophisticated black students they were supposed to be teaching. The new elite couldn't handle the "street niggers." The programs didn't function because there wasn't nothing there from the get-go, and around the second year, the whites started messing with the money and all we had left was utter confusion posing as black studies. It got so bad at one urban school that a sister confided in me and ended our conversation by saying that she wished a white boy would come in and straighten this mess out. That's real!

THE ULTIMATE REALIZATION:

The reality of the whole mess is that whatever is accomplished is still in the final analysis, the white boy's. Yes, he paid for it, so it is his. This is to say that if any competent Afrikan-American studies program comes out of Harvard, Yale, Cornell, Brown, or what have you, it belongs to those respective schools. This means all the time, energy and research that goes into the development of programs on white campuses are in the interests of the white boy, our supposed enemy. Oh yes, brothers can rationalize by saying "Well, black students will come to such and such school, so we should be there to direct and aid them." Now, no one can argue that point. My point is—is it worth the long range effects? At most, on any given white campus, you get five to eight per cent black students. This is to say that black studies should be where the majority of black students are—the black schools and black communities. After all, you don't go to Harvard or Fisk University to study Jewish studies, you go to Brandeis or Columbia. Right? The centers of Afrikan and Afrikan-American studies should be at black institutions.

In terms of white schools, there should be Afrikan-American studies societies or black student unions as well as courses integrated throughout the regular curriculum. Also, what is needed is that the white schools set up exchange programs with the black schools that have competent Afrikan-American programs. Why couldn't Harvard have exchange programs with the Institute of the Black World or another competent institution? If this was done, you would channel some of the much needed funds from Harvard and other white schools into the black community. But, most importantly, you are helping to build your own institutions, institutions that must be respected and listened to as you respect and listen to Harvard, Yale, etc.

A major setback is that few black people are psychologically or historically prepared to deal with themselves in the context of white schools—the failure and drop out rate is fantastic. Brothers and sisters who are really concerned should at this point also concentrate their efforts with pre-school through high school students. No doubt about it, we are ill-prepared; if there is any real expertise, let's get it into the primary levels. But there is little money there and almost no status! People will not call you professor—only brother.

We have to stop depending upon the white boy to define and legitimize us. To deal with our problem, alone by ourselves in the seventies, is innovative. We need original thinkers who can politically deal with the *right* and the *left* (is there really any ideological difference between William Buckley Jr. and Herbert Marcuse?). We need brothers and sisters who are hip to the world and are able to deal effectively with foreign policy and foreign affairs (How many brothers and sisters know about the *Council on Foreign Relations?* A 1,500 member New York organization—mainly bankers and lawyers—who meet periodically to "ponder" world affairs, or about the real relationship of Ford Motor Company to the State Department). Technology is the watchword. After all, General Motors makes more than cars. Think tanks are nothing new; they are just new to us. We've been a problem and therefore have merited study. We need Grier and Cobbs to study "white rage"; why doesn't Kenneth B. Clark do a study on white people?

When *The Report from Iron Mountain* was published in 1967, it was overlooked by most black people. However, in its conclusion it didn't overlook us. We are referred to in the *Report* as "undesirables," "minority groups," or "potential enemies." The *Report* put together by some mid-western scientists and thinkers studies the necessity and desirability of perpetual peace. What concerns us about the *Report* is that it suggests that in order to control the "undesirables" or "potential enemies" of society, a given society must consider "the re-introduction, in some form consistent with modern technology and political reality. The point is, if you're talking about modern technology, in most cases you don't need "concentration camps" or "barbed wire" or any other enclosed area. After all, we've had the most dangerous weapon of the twentieth century in our homes for the last twenty years—television! If you control a man's mind, you've got his body. And that's where most of our people's minds are—at a T.V. level. Also fifty-five per cent of black people in this country now live in urban areas. In Chicago where over a million of us exist, we're confined to less than twelve per cent of the land. This is to say that we're already concentrated.

Qualilty of life in the black community is already at an all time low. And our new elite, the *educated pimps* are in effect *very selfish slaves* being controlled by the same meaningless ideals and materialism that has been used throughout our history to control us. We now have professional black studies co-ordinators, brothers who travel the country setting up pseudo-black studies programs for anybody for a "modest" fee.

We have enough theoreticians, writers, poets, political scientists and the like; what we need is brothers and sisters who will put the theories into action—action out the writers' and poets' words along with the writers and poets themselves. We have enough leaders leading us no place. And yes, we know that we're a bad people; we so bad that we badly organized, badly situated and badly taught as we loosely talk about nationbuilding like its something that will jump out of the sky. If the white boy gave us a block tomorrow, we'd have problems running and organizing it.

We need a true building ideology (which will embody our spiritual and moral reality). We need to develop a standard of living compatible with the work that needs to be done. (If you make thirteen thousand dollars, you should be able to live off eight thousand dollars and put a good portion of the remaining five thousand into some constructive community effort.) Seek out and find brothers and sisters in your area who are trying to accomplish the real. Prepare yourself; widen your field, become the best. Remember you reflect what you are. You are the community and the community is you. In the final analysis, there is no difference between the Ph.D's and the pool players and we all need the study of blackness, the study of ourselves. Our problem is not that we don't realize that we have a problem; our problem is that we don't realize we all have the *same* problem.

LIFE-STUDIES

to hate one's self and one's people
is not normal
to perpetually wish to be like other people
is not normal
to act against one's self and one's community
is not normal
that
which is normal for us
will never be normal for us
as long as the abnormal   defines what
normality is.

From
Black Purpose
to Afrikan Reality

TO CREATE INSTITUTIONS, FOUR BASIC INGREDIENTS are needed: Work, Study, Creativity and Building. You cannot have one without the other. All four steps, if put into practice under the proper circumstances, form in the Afrikan man the nucleus of the basic building blocks of all Afrikan institutions. The nationalist who builds Afrikan institutions is the stimulator/innovator.

KUFANYA KAZI (To Work)

Nothing can be accomplished without hard work. When we talk about work in the black community, it is usually after the eight hours we've put in for the white boy. All work in the Afrikan community should be around the genuine needs and genuine wants of the black community, which means that you can't always do what *you* want to do—there are priorities. Just as we give the European-American eight hours a day, we *must* give ourselves eight or more hours a day. This is important because the European in his evil works three shifts a day, generally using other people to do his dirt for him. That is to say, we work one shift for him; on the second shift we talk about what other brothers and sisters are not doing and what *they* are supposed to be doing; and on the third shift we drink or smoke bush for about four hours, sleep four hours and get up and go to work the next day and wonder why we're behind. We're behind because we are not collectively serious about the *real* work that must be done in this world in order to achieve Self-Determination, Self-Respect and Self-Defense. This is no one man venture. Even though it may start with one man—you—we must organize and work within an organizational structure that is involved realistically in the black community. You can't do it by yourself. We must wipe out the need to individually *do our own thing.* No one man built anything. We must co-operate at the highest level of human involvement to help reconstruct the world for our children.

KUSOMA (To Study)

Work after a while ceases to have meaning if one doesn't understand the reasons why one works. Work is the practical application of knowledge. Knowledge is obtained by work and study. By working, we will be confronted with unforeseen problems; by studying, we begin, scientifically, to seek answers to our problems. With this kind of knowledge there is understanding and this knowledge is not divorced from the real world. Also, by working first we see that which is practically and realistically needed. Work will be a guide to that which needs to be studied. By studying the world of the past, we lower the possibilities of mistakes for the future. Study, an exercise for the mind, helps to advance our people intellectually and spiritually. To be aware of the problem is the first step toward solution of the problem.

KUUMBA (To Create)

Nothing is created in a vacuum. All creation comes from the world we're involved in. Some are needed and some are not needed. Creativity mainly involves the stimulation of the mind so as to move it from idea to practice. By *working* we see that which is practically and realistically needed in the Afrikan community. By *studying* we investigate methods used throughout the development of civilization as to apply those we can use to our situation. We combine that which we have learned from *working* and *studying* to come up with creative, viable and workable alternatives. You don't close yourself from the world to create for the world. That is why we say *work* and *study* in that order. If you find yourself cut off from reality and the necessities of black people, then you're probably creating for somebody else's world.

KUJENGA (To Build)

To build institutions is to physically construct thoughts and actions. You cannot institutionalize *thoughts* and *actions* at a *mass level without institutions* (whether they be formal or underground, you need a structure). To construct and build is not an end in itself, but one of the larger means toward the end that comes about because of *work, study* and *creativity* in schools, hospitals, community centers, co-operative businesses, parks, places of worship and so on. If this is done with the proper sense of sophistication, all that we will construct will move us toward self-reliance, will move us from being mass consumers to being mass producers for ourselves. In building, we *create* concrete models in the community that black people can relate to, respect and support. Building, whether a concrete and steel structure, or a plan of action that works, is desperately needed and is *one* of the larger means toward our common end which is the spiritual and cultural re-awakening of Afrikan people.

Work, Study, Creativity and Building will direct us toward the empowerment of the Afrikan world. Study and Creativity are the nation *planning*. Working and Building are the nation *becoming*.

Is it Best for Black People?

ONCE YOU HAVE REMOVED YOURSELF FROM THE BACK-ward and non-progress cult of the *individual* to that of the Afrikan man who understands and functions in relation to other Afrikan men in our communal (collective) tradition, your actions will be guided—consciously and unconsciously—by this question: is it best for Black people?

There is no individual anything. The entire European/capitalist philosophy of the worth of the individual over the collective body is always the major stumbling-block when trying to build black community organizations. Few black people understand their role in the context of group and national responsibility. All too often, their personal needs and desires take precedent over the needs and desires of the people—therefore the individual will move to accomplish that which is best for himself at the expense of the collective body.

No one individual builds anything; an individual may have had an idea, but to see the fruition of the idea, you need collective action. For example: no one white boy built IT & T to where it controls over seventy percent of the tele-electronics communications of Latin America; no one white boy built GM to the largest industrial nation-state in the world; in all of its evil and greed it took many Europeans who had a common identity, purpose, and direction. The only thing that the individual can accomplish by himself is to individually die.

Everything that we do—beneficial to Afrikan man, takes a collective effort and if it's not beneficial to Afrikan man, we should collectively question if we should be doing it. Once you understand this, and if you're working within an *Afrikan frame of reference,* with our own black cultural directives—automatically before you perform any act, you will ask yourself—*is it best for Black people?* Not is it best for Joe Blow, or Mary Williams individually—but will it ultimately benefit *us,* benefit the majority of Black people.

If you are talking about quality education, it shouldn't just be for your child, but all Afrikan children; if you are seeking higher living standards, it shouldn't be just for your family, but for all Afrikans. Your personal involvement must go beyond the selfish "my family first" attitude to the larger family of Afrikans. This is not easy—for we have been raised as selfish, individualist, ego-centered people; yet, we've survived such madness up to this point, and have not buckled under the pressure. If we understand the world, and what needs to be done, then we understand that a complete change in lifestyle is overdue. Remember, before you act—question yourself, *is it best for Black people?*

Mwalimu/ Mwanafunzi Relationship (Teacher/Student)

THE MWALIMU (TEACHER)-MWANAFUNZI (STUDENT) relationship is of major importance and must be understood and adhered to if an atmosphere of learning, discipline, and respect is to be created. In the final analysis, we're all students, but some of us have been students longer and have acquired a body of knowledge that must be passed on to those who are just entering formal life—studies: we call the teacher MWALIMU and the student being introduced to knowledge, we refer to as MWANAFUNZI. No institutions can advance intellectually, culturally, or politically unless there are dedicated and sincere MWALIMU with an equally committed WANAFUNZI. The Mwalimu and the Mwanafunzi are equally responsible to each other and must develop an unbreakable trust between themselves.

The following points should be observed by all Walimu:

1. Be the example of what you teach. Your personal contradictions can wipe out years of hard work. You must be direction for the young, be what you teach, exemplifying the Black Value System—"NGUZO SABA."

2. Always impart knowledge with an eye on reality. Pull your examples from the realworld that we're involved in daily. Highsounding philosophy belongs in philosophy classes that divorce themselves from life. Knowledge without understanding and practical application is like owning land without being able to cultivate it.

3. Never tire of teaching. An instructor who believes in what he's teaching can teach anywhere and at any time and is always prepared to teach; his lifestyle should be a lesson. Concentrate on the four ingredients for an Afrikan reality: to work, to study, to create, and to build.

4. The development of the moral, spiritual, and physical well-being of the students is of the uppermost imperative. A student should never be held back—in fact, a teacher should be eager for his student to surpass him; this is a reward for doing his job well.

5. In order to develop the communal spirit to the highest, the instructor must be conscious of and concerned about the student's well being outside the classroom. Make sure that the student has all basic needs in order to develop his mind, body, and spirit.

6. The student should be encouraged to investigate *all* areas of life-studies. The student should be given equal time and attention in accordnace with his personal ability. Push the complimentary and cooperative aspects of learning and encourage involvement with man and nature, and independent study. Never betray a trust, and discipline should be strict, quick, and fair.

7. All teaching should be based upon tradition and reason, and be taught theoretically and scientifically, the emphasis always on Afrikan man in relation to his community—community-centered rather than man-centered; emphasizing the responsibility of the students to their community, organization, and family; always communalism over commercialism.

WANAFUNZI (Students):

1. The student is the nation becoming. The good student never tires of learning. The secret of knowledge is that the good student can learn anything, anyplace, and anytime.

2. The good student is committed—committed to the institution/organization, committed to his people, and committed to the acquisition of knowledge that will aid his people—therefore aiding himself.

3. The good student lives the Black Value System—Nguzo Saba—and is the example for the younger brothers and sisters.

69

Mwanafunzi (students) learn traditional names of nations in Afrika. Books and magazines in the library as well as art work reflect a Pan Afrikan consciousness which teach the mwanafunzi who we are. Mwanafunzi above range in age from 2 to 6 years; mwanafunzi below range from 7 to 12 years.

KUUMBA. 2 to 6 year olds (above) dance after lesson in human anatomy.

Ndugu (below) stand at position of attention as a compliment to the intensity of the young brothers on the Jon Lockard painting overhead. Drummers from the community volunteer to work with the mwanafunzi.

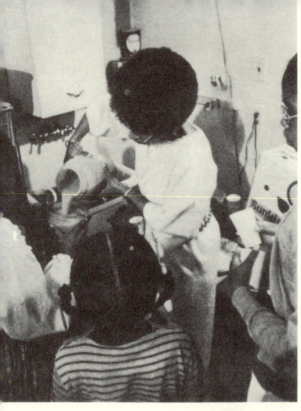

Chakula (food) Time. New Concept School is a community school which means parents are intimately involved with the school program.

Fresh fruits and fresh juices—such as carrot juice—are served and the older dada help to prepare the table while other mwanafunzi wash themselves before eating. Mwanafunzi above are 2 to 6 years old; Mwanafunzi at right are from 7 to 12 years old.

Three generations of Afrikan women, grandmother and granddaughter, exercise to be strong for Afrika and her many children.

At the end of the day (below), we direct our energies into Harambee (Let's pull together) for Afrikan People. Even Ndugu Khari (Kingly) who is 17 months old knows what time it is.

4. The good student knows that to move from black purpose to Afrikan Reality four ingredients are needed: Work, Study, Creativity, and Building.

5. Remember that a student's conduct outside the organization reflects the organization. To do injustice one day out of 365 days could wipe out the whole year's work.

6. The spirit of sharing and learning must be with the student at all times. But if he doesn't know anything—there will be nothing for him to share.

7. The student must develop good study habits, always show a willingness to learn, and always be respectful to the instructor. Address all male instructors with "sir" and all female instructors with "mam."

8. Knowledge without understanding and practical application is useless—if you don't understand something, ask questions. One who continually ask questions does not show stupidity or ignorance —he shows a thirst for knowledge. One who sits and absorbs everything without question is like a sponge—his head is full of water. Challenge your instructors to give you all the knowledge they have.

Money, Power, Sex: The European-American Corruptibles

OSAGYEFO KWAME NKRUMAH HAS STATED THAT "women, money, organized and obligatory religion, all three of them represent to my mind something that should play a minor part in man's life, for once one of them gets the upper hand, man becomes a slave and his personality is crushed." Osagyefo, in his usual down to earth manner, again hits at the core of our many problems. Yet, no problem is too difficult to handle with the right set of directives. There is an answer to every difficulty we face if we have the right value system and practice it with the same consistency we practice staying in style with the latest fads. We've found that without a workable value system of our own, out of survival-necessity, we have adopted wholesale the values of the oppressor and by definition position ourselves to be bought off very easily with the three European-American corruptibles: Money, Power and Sex.

MONEY:

Few blacks understand that everything in this world is political from literature to art, from what we eat to the air we breathe. In the economy under which we exist, capitalism, few blacks, if any, can ever acquire any real money or capital. Capitalism in this country and the world is controlled by few individuals and corporations. The major criteria for entrance into that exclusive club is to be European and rich. Notice I didn't say rich and European, thus ruling out all would be black capitalists because of the uniqueness and beauty of their color. The production and distribution of goods and services are controlled by these few blood suckers with the aid of government at the expense and detriment of the masses of the world's people. For example, this country can give a two-hundred and fifty-million dollar welfare check to the private aero-space industry and call it a subsidy; and for the little two hundred and fifty dollars a month check handed out to an unemployed father or mother, they make the receiver feel as if he is a criminal for not being able to find employment. The major pre-requisite for movement into a real money position is to be a person of European extraction. Yet, we are confused about what real money is, and its functions.

Most of us are aspiring capitalists rather than capitalists. The difference is that you can aspire to be something all your life, not realizing that your genetic make-up rules you automatically out of the definition. We're not even in the running, thus our failure from the get.

Actually we're bought off rather cheaply; not *ever* realizing what *real* money is we sell out for little or nothing because our value system is that of the individual over the collective body. We sell out for thirty thousand dollar jobs, federal grants, SBA loans, poverty program jobs, model city positions, cadillacs and any other mediocrity to pull us from the necessary work. For example, the president of GM makes approximately seven hundred and fifty thousand dollars a year plus stock options, expenses and many other benefits we have no knowledge of, and he doesn't even own the company; he's just an employee. This is to say that . . . he doesn't have any real money. No "negroes" in this world have a salary equal to that of the executive at I.T. & T. or GM.

However, the major problem with black people is that those who do get a little something become prisoners to it. In the ease of money—depending on the amount—one's whole life-style changes to a level "worthy" of one's new found riches. Most of us are defined—and do our own defining—from a very superficial exterior level. Whereas, the importance of a man is not measured in terms of the positive goods and services he possesses. Don't get me wrong, I don't *equate blackness* with *poverty,* but on the other hand I don't equate it with the lavish and selfish use of wealth.

If you are really talking about nation building, how can you justify living in a one hundred thousand dollar home, when most of our people live in sub-standard housing? If you're concerned about black people, how can you feel comfortable with two cadillacs and a closet-full of clothes that change every year? In this country *luxuries* have become *needs* at the expense of the majority of the world's population. Just because you work at GM doesn't mean that you have to buy GM products. In our bid to become "somebody" we became "something" and are playing games, and don't even know the rules, judges and the game we're playing.

POWER:

Bloods sell out for model city directorships, university positions, city council seats, executive positions in industry, assistant to the President, head niggers in civil rights organizations and much, much less. Few of us comprehend what power is vis-a-vis the world and none of us acquires a position that yields power. For example, we have a supreme court justice who removes himself from all black cases so as not to be accused of a conflict of interests, yet, no white judge does the same for the white cases. None of the black congressmen has an ideology that is black. So few are concerned about Afrika and Afrikan people. (Many can't even define Afrikan people.) The way most of them act and vote, one could easily mistake them for Jews or Anglo-Saxons. They have more concern for the survival of Israel and Ireland than for the survival of Afrika. They have no influence over foreign policy in relationship to Afrika. Their voices on domestic policy for blacks *are sad* and *compromising*. They've *all* been bought and sold by the Anglo-Saxon, Jewish, Italian mafias. Their value system—as other would-be power brokers—is the *acquisition* and *mis-use* of what little influence they have. We pity them. Power in the final analysis is the production and distribution of goods and services for a people. What goods and services have we received from our *power brokers?* We can't eat rhetoric and their words are daggers in our backs.

SEX:

There is an old saying in the state department that "if you can't get the nigger with money and position, throw a new left blond in on him; he'll give up the movement and his momma for her." That statement is not too far from the truth. Due to the lack of values, we have adopted wholesale the values of the white boy, and in his evil we have out done him. If the brother or sister is not corrupted by money and position, the next element they use is sex. From the use of white women and men to those who have special needs—homosexuals and lesbians to the ultra-perverted. This tactic has been used time and time again with our so-called civil rights leaders. Even today, we see that many of our spokesmen are married to white women or men. Many of our Afrikan diplomats are married to Europeans. Yet, we don't see any Rockefeller, Ford, DuPont or Mellon, etc., married to any blacks. Yet, we feel that we can obtain our freedom by marrying our enemies. That is nonsense. Talking black and sleeping white. We should know by now that the European-American will use any means in his power to maintain his domination over the world; and if it means using their women, they will be used. How else could twelve per cent of the world's population stay in power? Get hip to that, brother and sister! You don't obtain your freedom by loving your enemies to death. Anyway, if love was power, we'd rule the world. The brother generally defends his position with white women by saying that, well she is an individual—she is not like the rest—she is not the enemy. If the sister used the same logic and said of the white boy, he's an individual, he's not the enemy, we wouldn't have any enemies. But that kind of crazy logic comes from association with crazy people. You don't see any Jews marrying Arabs, do you? They are serious about their survival. Are we?

We hope that this helps you comprehend how the Europeans use the three corruptibles to continually divide and conquer us. If one does not develop a lifestyle that is consistent with our struggle, he opens himself up to all kinds of temptation and corruption. The minimum use of money and the products money buys for our personal use is absolutely necessary. If we're to be enslaved, let the idea of liberation for Afrika and Afrikans be the chains.

Occasionally, we see the European use all three of the corruptibles to buy a brother or sister off. That is extremely rare. Most of our people, due to a lack of identity or direction, sell out to one or two of the corruptibles because it is the "natural" thing to do. "Every man for himself" is prevalent among most Europeans. And, according to the European way of life, *it is right* and necessary for European people. And, to be honest, we must admit that *we all have a price.* Our price as Afrikans in America should be the total uncompromising liberation of Afrika and Afrikan people. Nothing less!

A Black Value System: Why the Nguzo Saba?

WE FINALLY RECOGNIZE THAT WE NEED A VALUE system for Afrikans in America. It has become increasingly clear that this value system must take into account the political, social, economic, spiritual and emotional crisis that we face in the western world. The Seven Principles of the Nguzo Saba as given to us by Maulana Ron Karenga is the most forceful beginning toward the development of a Black Value System that cuts across known religious and political systems. This is to say that if the Seven Principles are adopted, one could not be accused of being anti-religion, but Pro-Afrika. One with the Nguzo Saba could not be considered anti-socialism or anti-democracy because the Seven Principles incorporate all known religious and political systems and adopts them to our Afrikan selves.

The Nguzo Saba is based upon Afrikan tradition and reason. As Maulana puts it, "We draw from tradition our cultural foundation of values and institutions. But we realize that we cannot become activists and seek to return to a totally Afrikan past while being both in America as well as in the present. We also realize that we cannot totally transplant African Culture in an American context; therefore, we must adjust our traditions to fit and facilitate our movement in America." If we understand what Maulana is saying, this would wipe out all the premature criticism that we're totally re-adopting an Afrikan way of life without any examination or critical re-adjustment. This value system is "rational and modern enough in its orientation to allow the exchange of goods and services within the society (America) yet never become a reflection of it on the level of values and lifestyle."

The Seven Principles are the basic values of the US organization founded by Maulana Ron Karenga. The Nguzo Saba in its righteous direction and Pan-Afrikan scope has moved across this nation like honey giving energy to the brain. Of all the concepts that Maulana Karenga has initiated, the Seven Principles of the Black Value System is the most used. Most of the independent black institutions and all of the black nationalist organizations have used the Nguzo Saba in one way or another. However, it must be understood that the Seven Principles are only a part—a major part—of an entirely new system of revolutionary movement: Kawaida. With my limited knowledge, it is not for me, at this time, to attempt to teach the Kawaida movement. Yet, we must point out that the Seven Principles form the basic system of the values of Kawaida. Listed below are the Seven Principles of the Nguzo Saba:

UMOJA—Unity: To strive for and maintain unity in the family, community, nation and race.

KUJICHAGULIA—Self-Determination: To define ourselves, create for ourselves, and speak for ourselves.

UJIMA—Collective Work and Responsibility: To build and maintain our community together and make our brothers' and sisters' problems our problems and to solve them together.

UJAMAA—Cooperative Economics: To build and maintain our own stores, shops and other businesses and to profit from them together.

NIA—Purpose: To make as our collective vocation the building and developing of our community in order to restore our people to their traditional greatness.

KUUMBA—Creativity: To do always as much as we can in the way we can in order to leave our community more beautiful and beneficial that we inherited it.

IMANI—Faith: To believe with all our heart in our parents, our teachers, our leaders, our people, and the righteousness and victory of our struggle.

It must be noted that what we view here is only an introduction to the whole and if used properly the Nguzo Saba will definitely bring about change in one's personal life and organizational life. Serious study of the Seven Principles is *absolutely* necessary. You probably remember the old saying that a little knowledge misused is worse than a lot of knowledge not used at all. There are, at this time, no major texts that have been released to the public, but there are three books in print that we can lean heavily on; they are: *The Quotable Karenga* and the *Kitabu,* both published by the US Organization* and *Kawaida Studies: The New Nationalism* by Imamu Amiri Baraka, published by Third World Press of Chicago. All three are practical handbooks that are absolutely necessary for the beginner's understanding of the Nguzo Saba.

One last word, you can't just adopt one of the Seven Principles and get over. Maulana Karenga has stated that the Seven Principles are absolute which means that "nothing can be taken away from them, although there is always room for beneficial additions that do not duplicate the Seven Principles as they are already defined." To draw from the Nguzo Saba the principles that cause you no re-adjustment in your lifestyle is no commitment to the wholeness and soundness of the entire body. It is like eating only apples and thinking you'll live a healthy, sick-free life; just as apples need to be supplemented with other fruits and vegetables, the Black Value System must be taken in its entirety.

Each principle is protein that feeds the larger body. If you lose one element, the body weakens. For example, you can't just take KUUMBA (Creativity) and build a black theater movement on that principle alone. We need more than KUUMBA to operate a theater. What about the other areas that are necessary for the successful growth of black theater: finance, stagecraft such as lighting, sound and set design, publicity and advertisement, etc. What we're saying is that we need a value system that will govern *all* aspects of human involvement with the world. To accept KUUMBA without the other six Principles is like accepting an arm without the body; if the arm is disconnected from the body, you'll get a few seconds of use, but it will soon die because the arm can't stand alone. You need the body to reinforce the arm, just as we need each principle to reinforce the other. Each principle complements the other. To accept one without the other shows a deficiency in you, shows an unwillingness in the user to discipline himself to

---

*US Organization. 4302 Crenshaw Avenue, Los Angeles, California

a structure that might cause him a little personal discomfort because the value system demands a new commitment to the struggle, demands a new commitment to the collective community.

The Nguzo Saba is Pan-Afrikan in scope and values. All the values can be found in traditional Afrikan life. For the Nationalist not to recognize this and make some personal adjustments in his personal life-style tells us a great deal about him. Our communal commitment goes beyond the personal needs of one or two individuals to the needs and aspirations of the entire community. Can you adjust to that? We need a people who will think, act, live and relate to each other on a higher and much more functional level. This re-definition will by definition change our relationship to the western world. The major interference that the Nguzo Saba will cause will be to interfere with our powerlessness because we know that in the final come down, the one thing that the white boy fears most of all is black *organization* that contains identity, purpose and direction consistent with Afrikan survival. The European-American spends more money to keep us un-organized than he spends for all the model city and poverty programs in existence. Remember, the organized few can always deal with the un-organized masses (how else did the white boy get over?). Study and adjust to the Black Value System—it is a major step toward the unification and empowerment of Afrikan people.

Institutional Funding
a Word of Caution

THE VALUE SYSTEM WHICH WE'VE ADOPTED ENCOURages self-reliance. The Black Value System demands that we do for ourselves. The principle of Ujima—Collective Work and Responsibility—directs us to "build and maintain our community together and make our brothers' and sisters' problems our problems and to solve them together." The principle of Ujamaa—Cooperative Economics— directs us to "build and maintain our own stores, shops and other businesses and to profit from them together." If both principles are understood and adhered to, seeking major funding outside our own people is not acceptable. This is to say, *we will not allow outsiders to provide the dominant financial support* for our organizations. It is generally understood that he who butters your bread has some influence on your stomach.

We live in the most contradictory of situations. It is difficult, if not impossible, to move toward Co-operative Economics in a capitalistic system; it's like re-creating an Afrikan mind in a European setting. It is difficult to become self-reliant when the whole governmental system is against self-reliance. It is an uphill fight to develop a life-style of revolutionary consistency when life in the Western hemisphere is so systematically opposed to it and when this system displays its opposition materialistically and individualistically among its people at every level. It is a challenge to the mind and body to turn one's back on the European corruptibles: money, power and sex. It is the test of our time and our true commitment to *be* the positive example in all the tempting evil and corruption.

When talking about *independent institutions,* you have to be talking about *independent sources of funding.* The institutions, if they are to maintain their independence and autonomy, must be funded by the people themselves. Once, we step outside of this source, we endanger not only our credibility, but our independence too. For example, the Ford Foundation would be fools to give money to work against that which they stand for unless they can directly or indirectly benefit from that money. To them *all* money is an investment and few large foundations invest against themselves. We find that those who accept money from the big foundations and corporate structures run the danger of failure because in most cases their whole operation is dependent upon the money. However, the foundations get more mileage out of their "gift" than the recipients. For example by accepting let's say money from *Polaroid,* we by definition allow Polaroid to use us in their annual reports as a "black" group that they've helped. We, by association, help to justify all their evil and we also, again by association, legitimize the illegitimate. From the profits Polaroid takes from Azania (South Afrika) at the expense of our people, they give less than .005 per cent of 1 per cent of their annual take back to the African community. And we, by accepting their gifts allow ourselves to be used to the detriment of our people and our movement. Afrikan people don't want grants and gifts, we want our land back. A grant from big business that does business in Azani (South Afrika) is like a grant from the C.I.A. This can be carried on to other conclusions, but I'm sure you understand the direction in which we're heading.

Here are some suggestions for internal funding:

A. Your own staff should commit their finances, from 10 to 40 per cent of their annual salary, depending upon their family situation.

B. Enlist volunteer staff who should consistently give anywhere from 24 to 40 hours a week. This too depends upon their "other" jobs and family situations. For example, a single brother or sister should be able to give more time and money than a brother or sister with a family. However, those with families *should involve their families* too. This is important.

C. Use traditional methods (learn from the local churches) — rummage sales, bake sales, Sunday dinners, benefits to bring in national and local entertainers, anything that is *clean* and consistent with your value system.

D. A retail outlet (store, shop, restaurant) for selling whatever you can get your hands on is absolutely necessary. There are many independent black book publishers, brothers are now pressing their own records, clothing is being made by brothers and sisters and these and many other marketable items are available to *all* black independent outlets.

E. Try to develop a *product* that can be marketed locally and nationally (and internationally too). For example, if a black organization produces men's nationalist suits on the east coast, we shouldn't duplicate their efforts in the mid-west, but wholesale for them and produce something in our area that they can wholesale from us without duplication. This is how Afrikan nations do business. They aid each other by exchanging and selling each other's goods rather than trying to out-produce each other. This leads to co-operation rather than competition.

F. Develop any type of service-oriented business—laundromats, cleaners, barber shops, beauty shops, cab services, rug cleaning repair shops, etc.

Of course all my suggestions at this point are small, but are necessary for beginners. We cannot deal with international trade if we can't take care of trade within a square block of our communities. It is estimated that our GNP (monies which pass through our hands yearly—untouched) is 40 billion dollars. That money slides through our communities and slides right back out like it's on a greased rail. If black people, all 30-plus million of us put one dollar a year into a common fund, that would be 30 million dollars; if we put three dollars a year in a common fund, that would be 90 million dollars. With 90 million dollars, we could build quite a few life-giving and life-saving institutions and aid our brothers elsewhere. But, our major problem other than a lack of consciousness is who could we trust to administer 90 million dollars? That's why we advocate a value system where money is only *a means* toward an *end* and not an *end* in itself and all share fairly in the organizational returns. As Mwalimu Julius Nyerere has stated, "First and foremost . . . for our development we have to depend upon ourselves and our own resources. These resources are land and people." We have the people, we are about the business of re-capturing our minds so we can move together to recapture the land in Africa and wherever we are in the world.

The Natural Energy
for Positive Movement

MEDICINE (AND/OR MEDICAL CARE) IN THIS COUNTRY is mainly what is called curative medicine rather than preventive medicine; that is the medical profession tries to cure you after you become ill rather than try to prevent you from becoming ill. When one begins to think about it, the medical professions' calculated madness becomes clear. For example, the median wage of a doctor (M.D.) in this country is $41,000 a year; yet, the plain working man can't afford to go to the hospital for a week without fear of losing what little he has and getting deeper into debt. While, at the same time, most of these "pimp" doctors are busy buying their second summer house in the West Indies or Mexico.

This country is built upon human waste and the gross mis-use of its natural resources, i.e. to drink tap water here is as dangerous as drinking coffee or eating cake. One of the major industries of waste is the health business which is governed by the all-powerful American Medical Association (AMA), a very exclusive group of anglo-saxon gentlemen that function like a labor union, but with more sophistication. That is, we're charged more for less. You have undoubtedly heard of the military-industrial complex. There is also through the AMA the medical-industrial complex which includes doctors, dentists, pharmacists and all drug makers. Their major aim is to keep the public ignorant about preventive medicine such as organic foods (and brothers and sisters, the right type of life-giving and life-saving food is medicine/preventive medicine). The medical-industrial complex conspires to keep this and other information out of the hands of the people.

Black people are ripped off doubly. We have not only the AMA to deal with, but the new "black" poverty or "ghetto" doctors. There are the "brothers" who doctor in the community and live in another world. For example, through the use of medicaid and regular practice some of these "black" doctors net around $75,000 a year and one "black" doctor, Dr. Edward Williams of Washington, D.C., is reported to have grossed $300,000 in 1971 and after taxes took home around $215,000 while the infant mortality rate of blacks in the U.S.A. is about the highest in the world.

The major cause of illness in this country is insufficient diets. We have moved from real foods (organic and natural grown fruits and vegetables) to "foods" that contain additives, to "foods" that are processed, to "foods" that are chemically produced. We all eat from habit and that which tastes good, looks good and is easy to cook is generally what the American diet consists of. In most cases, we don't eat because we're hungry, we eat because the food is *there* and we're expectd to eat. And, we eat anything as long as it has been sanctioned by ABC, CBS and NBC or some black entertainer with a crown on his head.

Most of the human race does not consume large amounts of *meat*. Only the so-called civilized sections of the world are large meat eaters. For example, the North Vietnamese are winning a war and their major diet consists of organically grown rice and organically grown vegetables (when they can get them). Yet, it has been estimated by this country that it takes ten marines to deal with one Vietnamese soldier. And, the U.S. Marines eat three meals a day to the Vietnamese's one meal. Something is wrong with our diets because the strength and endurance of the near vegetarian Vietnamese far surpasses that of the meat eating U.S. Marine Corps. Toussaint L'Ouverture lived on berries and nuts and often *counseled his men on the proper foods*. It is not to eat more but what to eat less of. We should eat to live, not live to eat.

This is a country of overweight-undernourished psychotic people. If the average man misses a meal, nine out of ten he'll become sick, not because of missing the meal, but due to the psychological stress that is placed on him from feeling that missing that meal will in some way affect his health. *It will*—for the better! The superior diet is a frugitarian diet—that of fruits. Yet in this country, it is almost impossible to be a strict frugitarian. So we suggest a knowledgeable combination of fruits and vegetables. First, one must understand that fruits and vegetables are meals, and that all the nourishment that the body needs to function at its highest capacity is found in abundance in fruits and vegetables. How can man consider himself educated the way we mis-use our bodies? We're educated alright—for death and not for life.

In order for us to put in the extra eight hours needed in the community, we have to build our bodies to handle it. The frugal eater of the right foods will not only maintain his youth and vigor, but the sister will retain her beauty and figure. Both men and women will be able to function at a higher and more productive rate because the body will not be slowed down with unnecessary waste from bad food. This short article is not to try and win you over to a superior diet but only to make you aware of an alternative. The myths of high protein intake and the usefulness of milk are a wholesale farce. If you just restrain from eating bread, meats, eggs, milk, candy, pop for about two weeks and substitute these moderately with uncooked fruit and steamed vegetables, I'm sure you will notice a marked difference in the way you feel, function and look. Stay away from eating anything that is white: there are *no* natural foods in nature that are white. Any food that is white is a mutation of the natural. Foods like white flour, white milk, white sugar, white corn meal and white eggs are dead foods. (See Arnold Ehret's *Mucusless Diet Healing System.*) Give your body a rest. Eat less and fast. Fasting is the major way of cleansing the body. The old saying "you are what you eat" is not only true but is a warning for the undisciplined. If you see a brother or sister running around weighing 200 pounds or more talking about a new life style and black revolution, you know from the get that he couldn't be too serious because to be that large he has to have his face in some food at least three times a day for about four hours a day. With that kind of weight, he needs all kinds of sleep because his heart can't take it and his brain is always tired. The major setback is that food rules him rather than him ruling food. If he has become a slave to food, lesser temptations will undoubtedly turn his head, too. To abstain from certain foods not only disciplines you internally, but mentally too, makes you quicker and sharper. Proper food, brings proper weight and as we can say at IPE you don't lose weight, you lose waste. One of the major complaints is that "health" food is just another rip-off. It is if you are not careful and knowledgeable. As far as cost, how much is your health worth? We spend more on the upkeep of our cars than we do on our bodies. And, there is no way in the world that fruits and vegetables should cost more than meats, processed foods, and dairy products. Food is needed, but you must control food rather than let food control you. The only way to better health and more functional health is by logical and traditional use of foods which means that you'll be logical and traditional in the use of your body which will in turn serve you better. Pull that cigarette out of your mouth and check it out!

Ain't No Drug Problem in the Italian Community

OF ALL THE EUROPEANS IN THIS COUNTRY THE ITAL-ians are the only people without a serious drug problem in their community. The Italians are also the major distributors of drugs in the country. There is, in the Italian community, a rule against the use and distribution of drugs that is enforced to the letter by Italian men. Listed below are the three steps in their prevention program:

1. The first time we catch a pusher we'll issue a realist warning that generally works (this warning is for Italian pushers *only*).

2. If he has the stupidity to come back we'll break both his legs and shoot him up with his own stuff.

3. If he comes back again, obviously he is not taking us serious-ly or he has a serious deathwish. We'll make this wish come true.

The actions of the Italian men in their community may seem cold but *there is no drug problem in the Italian community.*

What are black men doing about the drug problem in the black community?

THE "BLACK ARTS"

WE ARE SOME FUNNY "BLACK ARTISTS"
AND EVERYBODY LAUGHS AT US

random house and double day publish the
"militant black writers"
who write real-bad about the
"money-hungry jew" and the "power-crazed irishman."
random house and double day will continue to publish the
"militant black writers"
while sending much of the profits received from the books by the
"militant black writers"
to Israel and Ireland to build a nation for the
"money-hungry jew" and the "power-crazed irishman"
while the
"militant black writers"
who write real-bad about white people
can't even get a current accounting of their
royalties from random house or double day
and black nation-building never crossed their minds.

The State of Black "Arts"
Is Only the Reflection of the
State of the Black "Artist"

TWO MAJOR FACTS BLACK "ARTISTS" (IMAGE-MAKERS —writers, photographers, film makers, dancers, musicians, actors, workers in the plastic arts, etc.) fail to face and focus their energies on in this country are the following: one, our lack of power and final control over our own "art" form, i.e., production and distribution—we create it and give it to the white boy to edit, produce and distribute; and two, our lack of concrete direction or purpose, that is we're all creators for different "personal" reasons and therefore only feel that we are accountable to ourselves as pseudo individuals and not to black people as a body. Each person's purpose for creating would cause major arguments among the "artists," yet, one fact is profoundly clear: We are an oppressed and colonized people (artists too) and have virtually no say-so over our own lives; we are *totally* dependent upon *other* people for our survival and everything else that takes us away from a recognition of that fact is secondary to our existence.

In our *individual* "artist" madness we have allowed the enemy to divide and use us against each other (witness Julius Lester's piece on "Nation-time? Late Again" in the fall issue of *Essence* Magazine, 1972). Yes, we as black "artists" exhibit our craziness in many ways; we give our people everything from Greenwich Village "hippiness" to "wipe the white boy out" revolutionary rhetoric. Actually, there is no general direction that our "image makers" are stepping toward that is consistent with the life and death struggle in which we are engaged. Again, *if you don't recognize a struggle, you don't struggle.*

The Honorable Sekou Toure has stated that "there is no place outside that (our) fight for the artist or for the intellectual who is not himself concerned with and completely at one with the people in the great battle of Afrika and suffering humanity." Where is the unity of our "artists" and "intellectuals?" As evidenced by some of the materials coming out, few of us know where the real, where the major fight is. Can you imagine artists and intellectuals in PAIGC (Afrikan Party for Independence of Guinea [Bissau] and Cape Verde Island) or FRELIMO (Mozambique Liberation Front) creating such madness as Sweetback's Badassss Song, Shaft, Super-fly, Guess Who's Coming to Dinner, 100 Rifles and all the other mind-destroying nonsense passed off as "black." Do you think that the Vietnamese people would allow and support such filth from their "artists?"

What is needed is a natural culture for Afrikans here (and worldwide) that speaks to our particular needs and struggle. We need to establish an international black thought so that we can begin to understand when a brother in Cape Town is hit we feel it in Chicago and at some level begin to move positively on that. We have more Negroes in this country worried about Jews in Russia than about brothers and sisters in these prisons in this country and Afrika. Where do we get our priorities from? Well, we get quite a few from the black "artist." He must begin to recognize that he is an influence and a reflection even though he may not want to see himself as one in a black context.

What we can move on right away is a national black communications conference to deal with the various tribes of "artists." This communications conference would bring together brothers and sisters from all spectrums of the communications field: from B.B. King to Leontyne Price, from Julius Lester to Imamu Baraka, from Charles White to Jeff Donaldson, from Roy De Carava to Fundi, from Melvin Van Peebles to Roy Capanella, from James Brown to

Aretha Franklin, from Isaac Hayes to Bill Withers, from Eddie Harris to Richard Abrams, from William Rasberry to Sam Yette. We can go on for days as to who needs to be there, but our survival (and that word has different connotations to different people, depending on their consciousness) dictates that we, at least, begin to establish some meaningful dialogue among ourselves.

The state of black "arts" is only a reflection of the state of the black artist and the black artist is only a reflection of the state of black people—that should tell use we're in bad shape. Let's move!

The Black Writer
and the Black Community

BLACK WRITERS ARE *FIRST* AND FOREMOST BLACK MEN and black women functioning within the context of their respective communities as writers, which is to say that they are black men and women of their community *first* and *writers* second. They are not writers who happen to be black, but are blacks who happen to write, thus understanding their fundamental relationship to their people. They don't, or shouldn't, relate to people of their community as writers (per se), but as another brother or sister fighting the same battle in the form they find best for themselves. *Writing.* Because, after all is said and done, writing is just another vocation like that of doctor, carpenter, historian, policeman, postal clerk, and carries with it its own responsibilities and importance.

Johari Amini has said that the black community is, "wherever they let us live." It is. And if you find that you somehow reside in a community where you are the "only one" or "one of a few"—maybe you'd better check yourself out because there is obviously something strange about you and your situation, for the majority of blacks in this country are in well-defined areas.

Images control our very lives (16 hours a day of ABC, CBS, & NBC does as much damage or more than the total educational system in this country). One doesn't have to go far to see the adverse effects of Julia, Mod Squad, Room 222, The Flip Wilson Show, The Bill Cosby Show, etc. We now get the American-style, the American-image in black face. So the important issues as a result of the mass media are *hot pants,* bell bottoms, hogs, hondas, night life, and other mediocrity to keep our minds off dealing with the killers of the world.

Have you ever asked yourself why is it that we don't control the space which we occupy? That's important! What do you reflect as you move throughout the world thinking that you own something—is it yourself or somebody you imagine you could or should be? You reflect that which influences you the most—if you are

95

acting white obviously white people have influenced you the greatest. If a brother is walking and singing like Tom Jones and Janis Joplin, obviously Tom Jones and Janis Joplin have influenced him the most. We understand that just because a "negro" acts crazy doesn't mean that he is, it just depends on who has been putting the pressure against his brain.

Black writers, as other black creators, deal in images. They understand the uses and manipulation of the image. One of the main reasons that our young so readily latch on to capsule form ideologies from outside the community is that black writers and others have failed. We have failed to give young brothers and sisters a workable and practical alternative in the language and style to which they can relate. We've failed to direct or set up and help operate constructive programs dealing with the *real* life issues on this planet.

Our first allegiance must be to the black media, that which exists and that which is to come. After all, the black magazines reach hundreds of thousands of black people weekly and monthly; the black newspapers are read by millions of black people daily. The "black" radio stations beam into the community 24 hours a day. The black writers could put some meaning, some positive stimulation between Diana Ross and Flip Wilson; could let the community know that there is more to us than illiterate disc jockeys whose only reading matter is wine commercials and rhyme books.

The responsibility of the black writer is great, greater when put into the context of so few speaking for so many. There are less than 300 black writers in this country that are published with any kind of regularity. 300 reflecting 35 million is deep—real deep. If our involvement as a people in the world is seen and understood properly by the writer, he could translate that knowledge into a form that black people could relate to and use. The black writer must be willing to give his *best*—free or at a minimal cost to the community; he must adopt a style of writing that will not alienate and turn brothers and sisters off. Must become the example of what he writes about. He must inform and help enlarge the perspective and world of the black community. Black people in this country do not have a tradition of reading *for reading's sake* and in most cases when we read it is not for pleasure or entertainment, but for information.

Most of us do not read as an intellectual exercise and do not need writers to play that game with us.

Sadly enough, some of our writers have become too well known and too important to deal with the "real" media in the community, have become too famous and *individualistic* to work in community organizations (if you are seen too much in the community, they might not think that you're really *important*). We have writers/ poets who think they are *stars* and demand a"star's" wages for them to breathe on us. This is for real; the worldrunners are going to the moon and the "negroes" are cleaning their cadillacs and talking about how bad they are, but some of us know that, like nations, stars fall every day.

Are Black Musicians Serious?

BLACK MUSIC AND BLACK DANCE ARE POSSIBLY THE oldest forms of "art" on this planet. Most certainly, for Afrikans in American, black music and dance are not only the oldest, but the most advanced and developed forms of creative expression that Afrikan people have retained in this country, i.e., the western hemisphere. Actually, the only indigenous "art" that this country has created has come from either the Afrikans or the "native" Indians. It has been historically documented that Afrikan music and dance played an important part in our total survival in this strange part of the world. Afrikans down through the ages have not only communicated with music, but used it as a weapon of deception (how could the slave be planning his escape if he always was singing and dancing?). We have used music and dance as ritual to put the departed to rest and to name the newborn. Music is the highlife of marriage between man and woman, is the medium to quiet the mind and soothe the nerves after a long day's work. Afrikans would not be Afrikans without music. Yet, Afrikans in America do not control their own musical art forms; we are not considered the authorities on our own creation and other people market our music like they market processed foods and homosexuality. We have let strangers make nightmares of our dreams, have let the enemies of the sun misuse the songs of our fathers.

One of the major short-comings of most black musicians is their inability to deal with the real world. Their inability, or non-willingness to negotiate with the actual world on terms that are beneficial to them as black men and women and as black musicians as a whole is a major shortcoming among many of them. There seems to be too much "individual" push and drive when trying to get *their personal* "thing" over—musically and creatively—but little effort, if any, is expended collectively organizing around their common problems as Black people who happen to be musicians.

One must understand and be able to define the enemy in order to systematically deal with him. Black musicians, quietly among themselves, berate the white boy and call him all kinds of weird names—but in the final analysis, give up with, "it's nothing I can do." And he's right—there is nothing he can do by himself; he must, with other musicians, begin to organize around their common needs and problems, must begin to organize around their future. One of the problems that confronts most black musicians is the lack of understanding of the major stimulus that motivates most whites that are involved in black music: money.

The black musician's inability to deal with the economic and business side of their profession has ruled them ineffective in the real world. This deficiency is not necessarily due to ignorance or stupidity of the economic and business world, but to the immediate priority—their music. In the end, their priority ends up being anti-music and anti-black. There is a saying among black musicians that is articulated in many ways—"we make it and they take it." Who own the record companies? White people. Who own the major publications that write about music? White people. Who own all the clubs? White people. Who have authored the so-called "major" texts on black music? White people. Who are the major record distributors? White people.

However, at some point in a man'e life, it becomes not enough to keep blowing hot air at the *man;* when do we as responsible people begin to critically assess the collective problem we face. After all, the white boy didn't force musicians to sign padded contracts—all he did was provide a pen. We, ultimately, at some level have to admit failure in doing the necessary homework. From the concert hall to the basement "jazz" clubs; from AM and FM radio to the airwaves of UHF and VHF: from record companies to record clubs; from the college concert to neighborhood jukeboxes—we have let Anglo-Saxons, Italians, and Jewish pimps dictate to our people what they must hear and what they must buy. We have let them, in effect, define what "soul" music is, thus mis-using it to the point that it has become legitimate in some "black" quarters to refer to the music of Tom Jones and Janis Joplin as "soul music." Don't laugh, it's just that serious.

On the whole, the black musicians in the 1970's have no one to blame but themselves; most of the black musicians that I've met live (all too often) in a world of their *own*. This world ranges from the very "spiritual" to the pseudo-intellectual to the all pervasive super-hip ending up with the mystic star rider—basing his whole future on his astrological chart. Their so-called *individuality* is equated with their talent or lack of talent, is equated with their freedom. He has to always do his *thang* at the expense of the group and sometimes the nation itself. Few groups stay together over a year or more; individual's ego and insecure personalities play a major part in their lack of collective security. I have met few musicians who are well schooled in the other life areas or art areas. They know little about black writing and writers, little about black art and artists; they voice school-boy theories about capitalism and talk about collective economics as long as they are unknown and don't have any real money coming in to be collective about. But after a couple of records, a few big club dates, they be back doing their *thang*—living their *now very private lives*. The formula is—when you have nothing, *share*, when you have something, *talk share*.

We find most black musicians politically naive, even in terms of their own interest; many don't even possess the sophistication to acquire a lawyer or agent who will negotiate contracts and club dates for them. Few understand their music in terms of a social and political force. And if they did, they, in their personal lives, act the exact opposite. The insecurity that exists among most *black creators* is astonishing. Just as the black writer didn't consider himself a writer until he was published by a major white house; just as the black artist (plastic arts, etc.) yielded to the large white galleries to legitimize his work (or what he thought was a legitimization of his work); just as black film makers who have been bought off by the major studios display their sick actions through instant directors, incompetent actors, Jewish writers, and an inaccurate and degrading view of the black community; just as the known black dance groups who don't dance in the community anymore, *all have,* with little effort, become the new pimps in the long line of blacks selling blacks to the lowest European-American bidder. And, as far as I'm concerned, these people are just as dangerous as the dope pusher. We can identify the pusher and build defenses against him; yet these new pimps push a much more subtle drug, that of the image. He who controls the image controls the mind. Their association with the enemy, as intimate as it is, only suggests one of several things: The musicians are 1) extremely naive, 2) totally ignorant and receiving bad advice, 3) just outright treacherous and would do anything for himself or herself at the expense of everybody else.

The positive side of the whole black music disaster is that we have learned much from what little black music we've received. Most black writers/poets, known and unknown—have at some time or another, given credit to black music for inspiration and direction. Black artists have, time and time again, used black music as a source for their growth and vision. Black music is the major impetus other than black life itself for the whole wealth of creativity that we possess. Black music is used at every level of human involvement in the black community. However, if black music is so advanced, why are black musicians so backwards and untogether? Well, I have many ideas, but I think it best that the *black man who is a musician* begin to answer the question himself, begin to define himself from his own perspective and worldview. Starting with the fact that he is a blackman first and a musician second, understanding that his problems are no greater or less than those of the average blackman who fights for survival daily. Most black musicians have refused to come together on a collective basis, nationwide, because of basic insecurities and problems of individuality, thus, by default, making them powerless within the eyes of the industry that our music builds. Jews control Jewish music. Italians control Italian music. Why is it that everybody gets a piece of us, except us? The fact that black music is one of the oldest and most advanced creative forces known to the world is fine, except that it aids our enemies more than it does us. No matter that black music is the most significant cultural expression that has been created in this country—that means *nothing,* if our enemies solidly maintain economic control over it—which enables them to maintain economic and· physical control over us—its creators. The way they have misused black music is only second to how the black musician has been messed-over. Yet in 1972, if we haven't come to the realization that a people must control its art—if it is to re-direct, and re-define, or re-focus minds—we deserve to be in the position that we're in.

Black Art/
the Politics
of Black Poetry

HOLD STILL AND CATCH THIS, SEIZE THE WORLD AS IT passes by while we emulate madness disguised as civilization as our enemies challenge the existence of God. There is no need to tell you that black people are human, we know that the pain of human feeling flows in our living veins every day as we close the insides of us in us. Did you know that genius passed through Harlem the first half of this century? The corner of 125th Street and Lenox Avenue has seen Afrika in its various shades: Marcus Garvey, James Weldon Johnson, Roland Hayes, W.E.B. DuBois, Claude McKay, Zora Neale Hurston, Charles S. Johnson, Paul Robeson, A. Philip Randolph, Charlie Parker, Adam Clayton Powell (Senior and Junior), J. A. Rodgers; and we can go on for days, the list of black minds that graced the streets of the "negro Mecca" is inexhaustible and too sad to recall.

All that wisdom, all that knowledge that came our way against immeasurable odds, left us with a community unfit for human consumption, which is to say that our inability to organize, mobilize and institutionalize needed change at the mass level is a profound comment on the resources of the enemy, a real comment on our inability to deal with the most effective organization of people in the world: European-Americans. They are not the worldrunner because of an accident of nature; they worked for it. We were Afrikans acting un-Afrikan. Even though in the black literary world James Weldon Johnson in his *The Book of American Negro Poetry* refers to us as "Aframericans" as early as 1922, somehow along the way we lost the memory. When we say we are Afrikans (or as some would put it, Afrikan-Americans—depends on your growth and perspective), we are actually acknowledging our existence in relationship to a continent (land) and a definite heritage, that of Afrikans. There is no such place as negroland and just as the term negro itself is a european fabrication, we Afrikans have been molded to fit that fabrication. A european imposed identity is an effective means of control. The more you imitate the enemy, the less you struggle against him; his values and aspiratians become yours and your actions reflect the direct opposite of your actual being.

The editor of *Black World* relates our position this way:

> Wherever Africans were dispersed in the Americas they were confronted, in one way or another, with the exploiting European presence which underlined the African past be degrading and distorting it. In most areas of the Americas, Africans have at times been characterized by pathetic attempts to reject their heritage, and millions have served the ends of self-degradation and white domination by gauging their own humanity by the yardstick of European morals, manners and mien. To these Africans in the Americas, it was easier to identify with even the faces and symbols of Asia than with the image of Africa.

Yet, if we face *reality,* face the honesty of our ancestors, we see in the words of the poet Charles Cobb the beginning of the end:

> Africans in the U.S. became colored, negro or american. In Africa itself with the advent of the conquest and colonization we see Senegalese, Nigerian, Ibo, Kenyan have become the preferred definitions. During World War II when britain was being bombed, the West Indian island of Barbados (hardly bigger than this page) sent a telegram to Winston Churchill saying "hold on Britain; Barbados is with you." If Louisiana had not been bought from the french, undoubtedly there would be brothers running around calling themselves "afro-french" and

believing themselves different from "Afro-americans." We find now large numbers of African people in the U.S., that we are deprived americans as opposed to Africans who were conquered and stolen from our land. Junebug Jabbo Jones has said, "we are like a maid in the house, in it, but not of it." *We are an African people* and must define the history, politics and culture of this reality within the framework of our interest as a people.

Slow readers will by now be asking themselves what has all this to do with black poetry? Actually, it's simple perspective. Start from the real, from the actual, and you will not get caught up with some confused "artist" running across the village with the devil, talking under his breath about "art for art's sake," a european myth invented to destroy the bright minds of our world. No need in documenting the destruction that concept has caused—just sit on the block and check the brothers and sisters slipping in and out telling our secrets to the world under the guise of being artists and not black. Yeah, they be a "credit to the race," bad credit.

We have a history of writers and writing. The Renaissance of Harlem was not a myth, just a wonder, yet incomplete in its goals and impact on the masses of blacks. It did leave us with ideas and a philosophy to grow on. Kenny J. Williams said that

> perhaps nowhere else in Negro American literature is the tendency to ignore an event more apparent literary movement which covered approximately ten years and involved more than a hundred writers and artists not to mention the untold numbers of sculptors and actors.

The writers of American history did that which was natural. They wrote and interpreted that portion of history that was important to them and their portion of history that was important to them and their lifestyle. Harlem and its Renaissance was ours to record and ours to remember. We failed to do the obvious and we now suffer for it. We didn't control our music because we didn't create recording companies and were unsophisticated in the copyright laws; we didn't control our literature because we didn't build any publishing companies and therefore depended on the enemy to publish us; we didn't control the minds of our youth because we felt that others were better equipped to do that, especially in the primary levels—thus we sent our cihldren, in many cases, to an early death. The fact is that the Harlem Renaissance produced few if any on-going, life-giving or life-saving institutions absolutely controlled and directed by black people.

The poets of the Sixties at their place in time recognized this fault and at one level lashed out with the force of the new birth just being spanked on the buttocks, and at a more sophisticated level of building for tomorrow. As I have said in *Dynamite Voices*, Vol. I:

> Blackart is a functional art; it is what the Nigerians call a collective art. It is committed to humanism; it commits the community, not just individuals. It commits the Black men to future which becomes present for him, an integral part of himself. The Black writer/artist works out of a concrete situation, his geography, his history. He uses materials at hand, the everyday things which give texture to his life. He rejects the anecdotal as uncommitting and insignificant. Blackart, like African art, is *perishable* and thus functional. For example, a Black poem is written not to be read and put aside, but to actually become a part of the giver and receiver. It must perform some function: move the emotions, become a part of the dance, or simply make one act. Whereas the work itself is perishable, the *style* and *spirit* of the creation are maintained and used and reused to produce new works. . . . Thus the people reflect the art and the art is the people. The interaction between the writer and himself, is essential to the aesthetics of Blackness. Still, it is impossible to define and categorize the Black aesthetic, you automatically limit it by excluding improvement, advancement and change. No one can really define the white aesthetic—even within the context of traditional western literature; every time a new European-American writer hits the scene, there is an alteration of the white-European aesthetic. Blackwriting, like other art forms practiced by black people, expresses our attitudes toward the world. The Black writer like the Black musician, will continue to define and legitimize his own meduim of expression.

To legitimize our own medium of expression is much more difficult than it sounds, especially if we are hit with european images at a complexity of levels from billboards on our roof tops to sixteen hours a day of weird white people on the air waves telling us to be them. But what is even worse is twenty-four hours of "brothers" on AM radio giving us lessons on how to rhyme without meaning while trying to sell us on the virtue of "rock." The poets felt the damage, the danger, and acted.

The work turned out by the poets had many concerns. Here are just five:

1. a discovery of Africa as a source for race pride
2. a use of Negro heroes and heroic epicodes from American history
3. Propaganda of protest
4. A treatment of the Negro masses (frequently of the folk, less often of the workers) with more understanding and less apology
5. franker and deeper self revelation. Some of this subject matter called for a romantic approach, some for a realistic.

Sterling Brown said the above words in 1937 whereas we would only add that the poets of the Sixties tried to give positive direction and to re-define the images of the oppressor.

The black poets became the doers, lived their own words. Most became noticed through the black media: *Black World, The Journal of Black Poetry*, Broadside Press, Third World Press, Jihad Productions, *Liberator, Freedomways, Soulbook, Nkombo, Nommo*, community newspapers, *Free Lance*, and others. And there were communicative vehicles that lived and died in the decade of the Sixties. Many of the poets were/are sincere and real, but some, after becoming known and "famous" were actually using what brother Kalamu Ya Salaam called "pop-gun rhetoric" shooting the white boy dead with a lot of words and then joining his organizations (Morrow, Dodd & Mead, *The New York Times, The New York Review of Books, The Nickle Review*, Random House, etc.) for the final kill. Or as Hoyt Fuller puts it:

> Most of the young ones began by attacking the "Establishment" and by declaring undying allegiance to the cause of revolution and Blackness. But then, after the first brush with fame and a taste of fortune (books published, $500-a-throw lectures on university campuses), they began to succumb to the lures of the

American ethic. They had spent heated moments excoriating the "Establishment" press and the critics and the publications, but now they turned to the *New York Times Book Review* as if their literary life or death depended upon it—just like the white writers. It turned out that they did not really believe in the inherent evil of the "establishment" institutions: what they really wanted was to be recognized by those institutions and to be admitted into the insiders' fraternity. Many of them reacted with disdain against the grass-roots publishers and publications coming out of the Black community, explaining in haughty terms (when they bothered to explain at all) that they had to place their works where money was available and, let's face it, where a kind word—or even a not so kind word—from a critic would rack up a couple thousand books sales in New York alone. And so began the Great Rationale. Protecting the Black image and disseminating Black ideas was one thing; but playing the right cards for acceptance and recognition with the "establishment" was quite another thing: after all, *even* a writer has to eat (well) and (properly) provide for his family.

Some of the black poets in their youth and inflated egoes could not deal with the solution because they were now sleeping with the problem.

THE POETS SPEAK

The poets of the Sixties talked history as does Dudley Randall in "Seeds of Revolution":

> The Revolution
> did not begin in 1966
> when Stokely raised his fist
> and shouted, Black Power
>
> Nor did it begin last year
> when you read Fanon
> and discovered you were black.
>
> The Revolution was going on
> when the first black
> leaped overboard
> to the sharks:
>
> . . .

When your father (whom you deplore)
pushed a broom
and your mother (whom you despise)
scrubbed kitchens
so you could go to school
and read Fanon.

The new group of word makers recognized that change could not come about unless they created a climate for change and brothers like Doughtry Long tried with lines like

Black people
have got to be Black
or sleep
into a dying
and forget
that each of them is a Sun-God
we've gotta listen
the chaos around us is deep

Gwendolyn Brooks who left Harper and Row for Broadside Press (as others not of her persuasion and beauty were leaving Broadside to go to Morrow and other whites—whoever would accept them—now) spoke of the young Afrikans "Who take today and jerk it out of joint/have made new underpinnings and a Head." And that Head was led in part by the young spiritual leader in New Ark, Imamu Baraka, who said in "The Nation Is Like Ourselves":

The nation is like our selves, together
seen in our various scenes, sets where ever we are
what ever we are doing, is what the nation
is
doing
or
not doing
is what the nation
is
being
or not being

We looked for tomorrow in the words of Jayne Cortez as she spoke of our "Initiation":

> During the season of cut organs we
> shot forward like teeth spokes from runaways
> a lost cargo of part flesh   part ash part
> copper & zinc
> sucking in names like katanga
> like congo
> we dissolved our chains

While Johari Amini woke us with her silence and creative use of language:

> hear our silence
> our silence
> and listen to the remembrance
> of our ancient selves
> ancient as we were
> selves echoed from the burned/gold prebeginnings
> of this now age
> from before the opening
> of this world into an earth
> listen
> listen through the sun
> through the essence sprung
> from what we once have been
> the once sun of our blackness
> propelled into a million midnight stars
> we will come
> we will come
> we will come
> once more

Most of the poets were Pan-Afrikanists/Nationalists or, more simply, black nationalists: people with a common past, a common present and working for a common future.

We exist in a country where a black unemployed family of four has difficulty obtaining a governmental subsidy of $250.00 a month (called welfare); yet in the same breath Congress gives Lockheed, one of the nation's largest aerospace/aircraft producers a subsidy (not called welfare) of $250 million dollars. The poets understood that if you play games and make up the rules also, your chances are much better for winning. Most recognized that their creations (their poetry) was their only bargaining point and that if they sold their creations, all they would be doing is duplicating the brothers and sisters of the Harlem Renaissance. They knew that one could not separate the literary from the ideological; everything in this country is political, from the drug addiction of a thirteen year old to the illiteracy of a grown man. Most understand that in the final analysis the *New York Review of Books* is just as dangerous as the *New York Times* and to publish in either is to legitimize the illegitimate and suggest that they are publications that black people should actively support.

Through the words and actions of Sonia Sanchez, Sterling Plumpp, Etheridge Knight, Keorapetse Kgositsile, Marvin X, Ahmed Alhamisi, Evertt Hoagland, Gwendolyn Brooks, Ed Bullins, Larry Neal and others, an atmosphere for a new day was built. The real work is yet to be started. Institution building is not an overnight process and takes more than the words of poets. Action must become part of our lifestyle. We say build like you dance and teach as well as you dress. Words are helpful and needed, but in 1971 negroes are still studying the stars (astrology) and the white boy is collecting rocks and driving dune buggies on the moon. My sign is Afrika and Afrikans; what's yours, brother?

The Necessity of Control: Publishing to Distribution

A SHORT PROPOSAL FOR BLACK DISTRIBUTORS

IDEOLOGICALLY AND POLITICALLY WE'RE TRYING TO break our total dependence upon European and Euro-American publishers and distributors. To publish our own books and to disseminate them in our own communities is one road toward self determination and self definition. It has become increasingly clear that if a book written by a black affronts the particular sensibilities of European or Euro-American publishers and distributors, one of several actions will be taken against that book: 1) the book will not be published; 2) the book will be published with a limited budget which results in the book being printed in limited quanties with few, if any, funds available for advertising—this in effect kills the book; if the book is published in this manner, there will be a deliberate attempt on the part of the distributor to systematically overlook the black bookstores and outlets. But the fact is that if the book is published, no matter that it isn't pushed, the publisher uses its publication to ward off any criticism of racism or disregard for the black public and writer. This brings us to the political reality of publishing and distribution. We now understand that everything that involves human participation in this country is political from My Fair Lady to Sweet Sweetback's Baadasssss Song to the air we breathe to the dangerous food we eat. The name of the game is control and if we do not control our product from manuscript to book to readers we are, in the final analysis, just talking to the wind.

There are many reasons we must begin to tighten up our distribution, other than the most obvious. Publishing is meaningless if one's books are not distributed. By dealing with white distributors we, in effect, legitimize their presence in our communities and relinquish control over our books once they leave our warehouses. (In Chicago no black distributors distribute the Irish newspaper or books in Irish communities.) Also, the distributor makes the final decision as to who will receive or *not* receive certain materials (it is no accident that we still have to go to the major white bookstores for many of the new black books that are published by European houses.) Can you imagine the white boy showing a willingness to distribute something like Robert Williams' *Negroes with Guns?* Only if there exists pervasive ignorance on their part! Another point to be considered is that all the contact and business that the white distributors negotiate in the black community only strengthens their economic position in our communities and the world. We inadvertently aid them in *their* growth and development at the expense of our own. For the most part the major distributors (Levy in Chicago, for example) control the magazine and book racks of all the major outlets in our community (they would include bookstores, drug stores, grocery stores, etc.). So we get in our community that which *they feel* belongs there, e.g., *National Enquirer, Inside News, True Romance, The National Insider, True Confession, Sexology* and on and on, which reflect not only what they think about us morally and intellectually as a people, but that which they feel we should feed our minds on; their sex, crime and violence syndromes should not be the directions within our communities. Remember if you control the image (ABC, CBS, NBC, *Time, Life,* billboards, 24 hour AM and FM radio, etc.), you control the mind. And, in the actual world, that's what it's all about. How do black people recapture the minds of black people so that we can be about the business of autonomy and self sufficiency? It is no secret that the mafia is behind most of the major distributing companies and the power of their influence is major. You may or may not remember when the *New York Times* decided to distribute its own paper in New York City and were stopped flat by the mafia-controlled distributors. All the distributors did was put a proposition to the various news stands and drug stores and subway stands that "they couldn't refuse," which was if you sell the *New York Times,* they would stop distributing everything else. This would leave the retailers with just the *New York Times* to sell and build their business on. The *New York Times* finally admitted that to set up their own distribution was fantasy and bad advice from the editorial room. It seems as though the same minds who were writing editorials were continuing in their consistency of functioning on misinformation and arrogance, thinking that the influence of the *New York Times* actually extended to the streets and that the people would come to their aid. This did not happen and the mafia is again distributing the *New York Times.* However, we recognize that the legality of the mafia and the First National Bank in our community are both illegal and that their thrust is based upon the manipulation of people and the raw use of power whether it comes in the guise of bombed out stores, wrecked trucks, burned news stands of city summons, eviction notices, plumbing/lighting/building violations. Our enemy is the same, is one—Europeans and European-Americans. And, this must be understood completely so that when we do business with them we realize that ultimately their interests are not our interests.

It is obvious that mass distribution is the major necessity in the success of a book other than the quality of the book itself. The mass sale of books for the black publishing houses should not just be a business, but should operate in as business-like way as possible: economically, efficiently, with a high degree of concern for the people who are trying to reach and influence. The mass sale and availability of books are important elements in the education of a people. With the advent of the paperback, books at a moderate cost became available to a greater number of persons. In fact, the paperback book industry has been called a revolution in itself. It is not unusual today for houses such as Bantam to issue a first run of one million copies or more. There is not only a need for mass distribution of such books but a desire which will steadily increase with availability and low cost of books.

What I propose for black publishers is that each publisher push and solicit sales for all the members of the Combined Black Publishers. By using the lists of all the members of Combined Black Publishers, we could give the salesman a superb listing and wide variety to offer to retailers. (Between Broadside Press, Drum and Spear Press, Third World Press and Jihad Productions there are about one hundred and sixty titles with such diverse authors as C. L. R. James, Gwendolyn Brooks, Imamu Amiri Baraka, Margaret Walker, St. Clair Drake, Norman Jordan, Hoyt W. Fuller, Keorapetse Kgositsile, Sam Greenlee, Ahmed Alhamisi, Margaret Danner, Sonia Sanchez, Sterling Plumpp, The Honorable Sekou Toure, and on and on. This listing includes not only books, but records, tapes, pamphlets, posters and broadsides.) For example, Third World Press would train a salesman in the Chicago and mid-western region. His responsibility would be that of selling not only Third World Press' books, but those of all the publishers belonging to Combined Black Publishers. Normally, if we went to a white wholesaler or distributor, they would demand anywhere from 50 to 60 percent off the top and we still wouldn't have any guarantee that our books would be distributed in the black community. Our salesman would develop a man to manager contact and give us the person-to-person influence that is badly needed among black publishers. Rather than give the white boy 50% to 60% off the top, we'll give our salesman the standard 40% to work with the retailers. He would take orders for all the Combined Black Publishers and write them up and send them to the respective publishers and bill for himself a 10% commission off the list price for each title sold. The respective publishers would fill the orders and bill the retailers from their houses. Broadside Press and Third World Press would distribute in the mid-western region, Drum and Spear in the Washington, D.C. area, Jihad in the New York-New Jersey area, and so on. As we add new members and new outlets, we'll grow in those respective areas.

Phase two of my plan would be to actually stock and store all titles in each region. For instance when a publisher of the Combined Black Publishers published a book they would automatically send copies to each region. Of course when we go into this it would necessitate acquiring storage space equipment for distribution (mainly trucks) and organized personnel who would also be concerned about public relations and personalized displays for each title. This operation is much more intricate but needed if we're ever going to compete and hold our own. Phase two would call for mass distribution which necessitates mass publishing. And, the publishers could mass print with the right type of distribution. Mass printing would, in effect, bring down the unit cost of printing for each book, and would save money all the way around. The distribution would aid in completing advertising and custom marketing. Market research would determine what black people want and need.) And, of course, the best advertisement for a product is for it to be seen everyplace—bookstores, drug stores, barber shops, beauty shops, bus stops, bus stations, airports, school bookstores and libraries. This is a major operation that requires major financing and advance planning. This is what we're working toward. Our salesman would be not only selling books, but seeking new alternatives and avenues for our product.s

That too is why ideology is so important. A salesman must have direction and his motivation should not be based solely on profit and money. And I submit that if money is the reason we're in business, we're fighting a losing battle from the get. We are, in the final analysis, service-oriented businesses and must at a larger level channel profits we earn back into our communities to bring about a better and more productive and knowledgeable way of life for our people. After all, most of us started publishing because of a serious and sincere desire to inform our people. In the process we learned what "capitalism" and "aggressive competition" is all about. We learned that *to do* is more than just *to say* and regardless of how high your motives are, the name of the game is *money*. We *must* be conscious of this and not let ourselves be put into a non-negotiable position. Like Ted Joans has said, the white boy's real mother is money and he'll do anything for it, even sell his mother.

This is not our position. Our position is one of service and credibility. We now know that we're not competing with Random House and Doubleday, but with forces more powerful with unlimited resources and the only way we can survive and grow is to be solidly based in the community we're trying to reach so that *they* know and *we* know that our ultimate struggle is one and the same and that our race for life is partially determined upon our definition of death.

WORLDVIEW:

fact is stranger than fiction
here in America in the year of 1973
many black people don't even know how
we came to this land

some black people believe that
we were the first people
to fly
and that we came first class.

Europe and Afrika:
A Poet's View

WHERE ON THIS EARTH HAVE EUROPEANS VENTURED and not left corruption, disease, racism, classism and death in their wake? Does there exist a race of people who've been colonized by Europeans who have found happiness with the European presence? Has any nation whether Afrikan, Asian, Indian, etc., not suffered dearly at the hands of Europeans, and now, also, at the hands of European-Americans. The Europeans' rationale for their unwanted existence on foreign soil falls under the guise of bringing democratic civilization and Christian enlightenment to the "savages." Wherever the western white man docked his ships, he was greeted with warmth, friendship and unusual humanity as if this European were "civilized and cultured," but without exception, this same "civilized and cultured" being turned on his host with the highest form of trickery and evil, to the extent of completely subjugating the indigenous people as if the hosts were the barbarians. The Europeans' subtle treachery and self-appointed righteousness have not left room on this planet for other lifestyles or "ways of life" that are not consistent with the western concept of how man should live. This must be understood.

During the Fifteenth and Sixteenth centuries (after the modern Afrikan slave trade had started), European nations individually and collectively made some deliberate and systematic

123

decisions in terms of their own existence of which the major decision was to conquer the known world and as one historian observed, "whether it be flat or round we will take it." That decision to take the world may sound cold, but being only six to eight per cent of the world's population, one would have to be cold and desperate to even entertain such an idea. Motivated by Christian competition and natural aggressiveness, the British, French, Belgium, Dutch, Portuguese and German nations began to intensify their own brand of nationalism and sought out areas other than Europe for exploitation and exploration. Afrika was the logical choice, especially after the crusades (1100-1300 A.D.) where Europeans were introduced to civilization at its highest. That course that Europeans set for themselves at that time developed into a pattern which they follow to this day: the ability to challenge the known and the unknown regardless of what the price may be; after all, who were the first to challenge the existence of a God?

This is not the time nor the place to talk about nationalism, but we must understand that European nations and European nationalism went together like fish and water, like white and Europe. in their colonization of other peoples. For example, the various nations—British, French, Dutch, Portuguese, Belgian, and German —had certain similiarities working within their respective states that paralleled and interacted with each other: 1) a common value system which, at this time, had much to do with Christianity (Catholicism and Protestantism); a national language which they used to communicate verbally and on the written page; national cultural patterns which dictated dress, music, literature, dance and other cultural traits that forge people together and raise them to the necessary group and national consciousness; 2) *common purpose* which was, in part, to expand their empires beyond their national borders, to enlarge their national treasuries and to search for vital natural resources that were either non-existent in Europe or just on the verge of extinction in Europe, 3) important advancements in technology, especially in communication, transportation (within and outside of national boundaries, most notably in shipping), and warfare; 4) modern organization—each nation within its own perception of the world was organized to deal with that world. These new patterns of organization were most evident in government, business, and the military. This situation ultimately proved that the organized minority—as the Europeans were and *are*—can, under the proper circumstances vanquish the un-organized majority. Another important factor that is largely overlooked during Europe's expansion is the state of the world at that time. The Asian, Indian and Afrikan nations were undergoing forced and natural migrations, were experiencing change and re-organization and it was due, mainly, to this migration, confusion, and in-fighting that enabled the outside western white man in a matter of a century or so to conquer the world.

The absolute control of Afrika didn't come until the late Nineteenth and early Twentieth centuries. This period is commonly described by European historians as the "Scramble for Afrika" and by Afrikan historians as the "Rape of Afrika." The major European powers led by Leopold II of Belgium (he founded the International Association for the Exploration and Civilization of Central Afrika in 1876) established their economic, political, military and social control over all of Afrika with the possible "exceptions" of Ethiopia and Liberia (American controlled). The major impetus for this modern "scramble" was the Berlin West Afrikan Conference of 1884-85 where Henry Stanley made his famous "Dark Continent" comments and helped awaken the European population to the importance and significance of Afrika. This conference was presided over by Bismarck and was attended by all the major European powers, and, of course, the United States. This period in European history is of the utmost importance in aiding us in trying to understand the European conscience. Shortly after the "word was given" in Berlin, the various participants actively partitioned off and inhumanely "took" Afrika and to this day control the richest continent on the face of the earth with unheard of brutality and arrogance known only to the western white mind.

During the 1950's and 1960's many of the Afrikan nations that were created by Europeans and that had European imposed borders were given "paper" independence. What actually occurred was a formal changing of flags and a replacement of European government officials with "safe" Afrikan officials that still left Afrikan people with little economic and military autonomy. The notable exceptions are possibly Guinea, Algeria and Tanzania. The new condition set up by the Europeans in relationship to the new Afrikan nations is described by Osagyefo Kwame Nkrumah as neo-colonialism where physically the Europeans relinquish their presence but very subtly tie up their former colonies economically in the Western Common Market. (What the West did to the price of Ghanaian cocoa during Nkrumah's leadership is an excellent example.) Thus, if the various Afrikan nations are not internally self-sufficient and self-reliant (which means that as nations within their own borders they could produce and manufacture the vital goods and services that the people needed) a new and much more damaging relationship between Europe and Afrika will result, damaging because Afrikans themselves are now visibly and physically "in control" of the normal functions of government and cannot, necessarily, blame Europeans for the failure of said governments to meet the needs of the people as was the case during actual colonization. Since the Europeans are not in physical control, it is difficult to prove to the layman that the Europeans are seventy-five to ninety per cent of the time at fault. The responsibility of failure still falls on the most visible element. All the people understand is that they are now ruled by their own, but in many cases, the people do not understand the intricacies of running a country. Not only do the people not understand the changes and complexities of the new domestic policy, but few, even those Afrikans who are the new pilots of the nation, understand the interdependency of nations and generally end up re-selling their souls in a search for a meaningful foreign policy, too.

The current foreign policy of Europe toward Afrika brings us to our focal point. The countries of Azania (South Afrika), Zimbabwe (Rhodesia), Namibia (Southwest Afrika), Angola and Mozambique are still under the physical and military domination of European whites. In the countries mentioned there are approximately thirty million Afrikans under the whip-lash of 5.5 million Europeans. For example, Zimbabwe (known as Rhodesia), where less than 300,000 Europeans under the leadership of Ian Smith are now, along with the British, trying to make the five million indigenous Afrikans into their "negroes." There, we have foreign intruders negotiating the human rights and freedom of the rightful owners of the land. The minority unlawfully imposing their will upon the majority—doesn't sound very democratic, does it? Can you imagine less than 300,000 Afrikans in Britain imposing their will on the whites of London?

In Zimbabwe and Azania, the whites have proclaimed over eighty-five per cent of the Afrikans' land to be "white." One can easily understand this action knowing the value of such untouched and fertile soil, containing such vital resources as diamonds, manganese, gold, uranium, coal, oil, chrome and much more. The issue in Afrika as elsewhere is who will control the LAND. "Land is the only thing that nobody, no where is making any more of" and the Europeans are aware of this and are feverishly trying to tighten their grips on the last vestiges of useful earth.

Yet, the cold unforgettable fact is that no European power would allow itself to remain in a situation where it would accept rule by foreign minority, especially if that minority were of another race. That this situation for Europeans does not exist any place in the world today only underscores the observation that it is no *accident of nature* that, wherever Europeans and people of color exist together in the same space, the Europeans *rule* and the others are *ruled*. It must be understood that it is no trick of fate that keeps European people in power but a common determination to stay there. John H. Clarke puts it this way:

> "European people, within Europe and in the broader world outside of Europe, have always maintained their power and control with a form of protracted violence. The humanity and naivete of Afrikan people seem to have always interfered with their understanding of this point."

History has shown that Europeans do not even accept rule by other Europeans. Examples of this are the French Revolution, America's war with Britain, the First and Second European Wars. The most obvious aspects of this can be seen also today in the tribal war in Belfast between Protestants whites and Catholic whites.

Whereas, religion and ideology have sometimes in the past been the causes of war and conflict, we now agree with W. E. B. DuBois and others who have warned that *race* will be the tearing factor of the Twentieth Century. If Europeans will not adjust themselves to rulership by a foreign body under any circumstances—Europe for Europeans—this leaves us to conclude, using their logic, that Afrika should be for Afrikans. In our minds, this is the issue. Afrika for Afrikan people whether in Zimbabwe, Guinea, Azania, Namibia, Tanzania or elsewhere.

Brother Chancellor Williams, Howard University professor of History and the respected author of *The Destruction of Black Civilization* has defined in no uncertain terms who the enemy of the black man is:

> "I have said, reading from the pages of 6,000 years of history, that the whites are the implacable foe, the traditional and ever-lasting enemy of the blacks. There will be a beginning of wisdom and a possible solution of the problem when—and only when, blacks fully realize this central fact in their lives: *The white man is their bitter enemy.* This is not the ranting of wildeyed militancy, but the claim and unmistakable verdict of several thousand years of documented history. Even the sample case-study of the 10 black states in this work *The Destruction of Black Civilization* shows that each and every one of them was destroyed by whites. Facing this reality does not call for increasing hatred, or screaming and utterly futile denunciations. Far from it. For all these shouting, emotional outbursts by blacks are in themselves indications of weakness, because they becloud the mind and prevent the calm and clear thinking that is absolutely required for planning if the race is to be saved from final destruction. "Destruction" is not too strong a term here. Only fools will be unable to see that the race is again being hemmed in, surrounded by its enemies, and cannot survive forever under what might be called a state of gradual siege. Those "Negroes" who are still pleading with the whites for brotherhood through "integration" are so deaf and blind that they are unable to get the white man's message."

Brother Williams and others such as Marcus Garvey, Osagyefo Kwame Nkrumah, Patrice Lumumba, Carter G. Woodson, Oginga Odinga, W.E.B. DuBois, C.L.R. James, George Padmore, The

Honorable Elijah Muhammad, President Sekou Toure, President Julius Nyerere and Imamu Baraka have clearly defined our situation and the reasons we exist in this world as we now do; and their warnings are not a call for foolish, unthinking re-action, but a call for deliberate and systematic action with black purpose and direction underscored with the major impetus that is required in any peoples' struggle—the love of a people for self. The future of our children is at stake and to accept less is to compromise our manhood which is in essence to compromise our right to life itself.

Afrikan Love

OUR MOVE IS BACK TOWARD THE EXTENDED FAMILY,
back toward the humanistic involvement of families with families,
where no child is without a mother or father and no grandparent
is without a son or daughter, where *all* is shared and we take care
of each other. The basis of our family, as is our struggle, is *love;*
the love of our children, the love of our ancestors; the love of our
land, the love of the living Afrikans. That which harms a brother
or sister in Zimbabwe should touch brothers and sisters in the
Americas, should touch brothers and sisters in the diaspora. The
extended family concept is built around *human needs* and not the
material needs of humans. In Swahili this concept of familyhood
is called Ujamaa.

Our selfishness and individualism is the cause for much of the
cold in the Afrikan world today. We don't feel anymore. It seems
as though all our energies are directed toward "making it." This
is serious because it takes us away from the real problems and
humanistic needs of the majority of the world's people. One of the
methods that can be used for re-gaining the love we once had for
each other is continuous and realistic *work* (Kazi) in the black
community, especially with black children. If there is love in you,
our children will bring it out. If there is no love in you, our
children will make you feel some.

131

Our struggle should not be based upon the *hate* of anything, but the love of life and our people. If we have the necessary love, by definition anything that upsets our way of life we're automatically against and will fight to the *win*. One cannot build a movement on the negative. One cannot sustain a struggle on the anti. Our fight by definition should not be anti European-Americans, anti-capitalism or anti-white, but should be pro-Pan-Afrikanism, pro-Ujamaa (Co-Operative Economics) and pro-black people. This way we create a frame of reference where as we are defining and acting in the positive rather than being defined by and re-acting to the negative. By using our own frame of reference, we are giving alternative direction and introducing new values.

Nobody can define the needs of Afrikans but Afrikans. We don't see Afrikans in Sweden telling the Swedes how to run their lives! So, we too must define the direction that we must go ourselves. The Honorable Sekou Toure has stated that "You either serve the people or you use the people." There is no in-between. If genuine love exists and is passed on among our people, for a child to serve the community will not only be in keeping with the dictates of the black value system, but for the child, this would be an honor and privilege. This would be one of the ways that our sons and daughters acknowledge their thanks to their ancestors, their families and community for benefits that they enjoy in their youth and will continue to enjoy as they grow and mature.

The love that members of the Afrikan society reflect for the people of their society is something that is mis-understood and foreign to the European's way of life. It's like acupuncture is to the western doctor. It cannot be co-opted and taught in eight easy lessons. So the A.M.A. put a ban on it. The West has put a ban on Afrikans' getting together, thus aborting any love base to re-develop. Our love and responsibility to each other should be a *way of life* and must be taught from birth. The life-style that we develop must be one of warmth and substance. Warmth: the ability to smile and touch the inner core of our people as to radiate a sense of security, completeness and substance; the ability to offer a new reality, a new competence that successfully follows through on all projects; also the ability to transmit within our world a feeling of confidence and security in our own worth and actions. The Vietnamese people are winning because they have warmth and substance in their righteous struggle; FRELIMO will re-gain their land because they generate warmth and substance in their daily fight. They are fighting *for* their people and by definition against their enemies—we accent the positive.

The love for our people should be so deep and clean that a verbalization of it becomes unnecessary, although at times expected. Our very actions, our life-style must exemplify such a spirit. Our love must be so unshaking that it stands the test of the European corruptibles: money, power and sex. We must be so positive in our attitude toward each other that we never, never consciously or unconsciously, under any circumstances, take advantage of another brother or sister. I don't care if the niggers think that they are super-slick! That's alright, because they're going to run up against the real-slick ones sooner or later. We must concentrate on the *positive,* on the constructive. Too often in our *blackness* we're so bad that we scare our own people away. Our people fear us more than the white boy. We must be aware of this. There is an old Afrikan proverb that says "We must cure the illness without killing the patient." We are now at war for the minds of our people.

The relationship between man and man, man and woman, man and children will be clarified and re-defined once the black man and woman involve themselves in the genuine struggle of the black world. As long as they remain apart from it, doing their *own* thang, by definition, *our* thang will never be completed.

The black woman to us is something extra special. Special, not in the sense that we should crown her queen and put her on a pedestal, but to understand that we have *no* future without her. She as a complimentary force working at our sides reinforces us when we weaken and doubt the correctness of our struggle. The black woman and the black man, should recognize that in terms of tradition and family association, each has different roles to complete: a woman cannot be a father and a man cannot be a mother; *they may substitute* but will never fulfill those special roles.

At this time in our lives, we seem to be threatened by each

133

other. That is to say that we've internalized the values and aspirations of our enemies to the point that our relationships with each other are sometimes strained and frustrating. The root of this is that we've become so acculturated to the European way of life that the change over from Afrikan to European-American has left us very insecure as a people. We're so insecure in our manhood and womanhood that a *continuous re-assertion* of a European individualism vis-a-vis man and woman inadvertently has made us antagonists. Black man against black man; black man against black woman; black woman against black woman; black woman against black man. All this stems from the European definition of man and and woman which is based upon material possession and superficial exterior rather than the human basis of Afrikan man and woman.

This is sad. Black men are being ripped off daily in Vietnam, in the prisons and in numerous other death traps invented to separate us from the real world. It has been estimated that black women outnumber black men two and one-half to one and that dealing with that fact emotionally has driven black men and women further apart seeking answers where they cannot be found. You you cannot solve a family problem when you're not even defined as a family.

The extended family concept solves many problems. First, that of security. When one eats, all eat. If one has a house to live in, all have a house to live in. When one works, all who are physically able work. Most of the needs of the members of the family are met by the family, such as care for the aged, seeing that all children have a mother and father, quality education available for all the children and not just those who can afford such. This family structure allows you to pool your resources, thus making your bargaining power greater. For example, if there are fifty members in your community-family—if you got hair cuts at a special barber shop, we're sure you could get a special rate; if all of the family members used a special cleaners for their clothing; again, a more economical rate. There are all kinds of possibilities in this and all kind of dangers if not operated within the correct value system and Afrikan frame of reference.

Basically, the extended family is the beginning of the extended organization. As with the family, a *new* and lasting trust is built which will enable its participants to function at the highest of their ability. This concept of shared and complimentary work and study over that of personal possession and individual aggressiveness is the beginning of the solution to our many problems. Collective eating brings collective working; collective working brings collective thinking; collective thinking brings collective action; collective action brings results for the collective body. The future of our children is at stake.

> catch that smile, return it
> share that food, you've earned it
> know your brother, build on it
> help your sisters, make a way of life of it
> teach our children, by being it
> create your life
> around the love of it

White Racism:
A Defense Mechanism
for Ultimate Evil

IF THERE EXISTED A VOID IN A PEOPLE AND THE PEOPLE
were knowledgeable of it and if this void was important to their existence, common sense would dictate that they fill such a void, if possible. If it were not possible to fill such a void, a people, in order to
sustain their well-being, in all likelihood, would develop a substitute
for the void, or a defense mechanism to meet their particular needs.
If you are thirsty, you seek water; if you are hungry, you seek food.
Water and food are absolutely necessary for human survival and
therefore must be obtained at any cost. There are psychological foods
that are necessary for human survival too: love, security, self-determination, self-awareness, self-respect, friendship, etc. How one defines oneself in relation to the world dictates how one functions in
the world. The working definition is important. Johari Amini has
stated that a working definition is a determinant of behavior. If you
define yourself vis-a-vis white people, your actions will be measured
from a white frame of reference. If your existence/definition is based
upon a white frame of reference, by logic, if white people didn't
exist, you would not exist either.

137

What would you do if you discovered that your people were only 9% of the world's population and that everybody else in the world not only outnumbered you, in terms of population, but *all* possessed some degree of color? To be small in number is bad enough, but to exist in a world of *color* without color, is odd, unusual, and strange. If 91% of the world's population all had some degree of color and were many in number, wouldn't those without color and small in number be left out, in a vacuum, or somehow existing in a void? The West, mainly Europe, has tried to define the world from its perspective, and has largely been successful in changing the standard of definition from the local (the Afrikan, Asian, Indian) to the European, which is, again, defined by Europeans as Universal.

Let's look at color. Dr. Frances Cress Welsing of the Howard University College of Medicine states in her booklet *The Cress Theory of Color Confrontation:* "'White' itself, or the quality of 'whiteness' (is) indeed not a color but, more correctly, the very absence of any ability to produce color. The quality of whiteness is indeed a genetic inadequacy of a relative genetic deficiency state or disease based upon the genetic inability to produce the skin pigments of melanin which are responsible for all skin coloration. The massive majority of the world's people are not so afflicted, suggesting that the state of color is the norm for human beings and that the state of color absence is abnormal. This state of color absence acts always as a genetic recessive to the dominant genetic factor of color production. Color always annihilates phenotypically and genetically speaking, the non-color, white." To carry Dr. Welsing's thesis to its logical conclusion is to state that the black man, who possesses the "greatest color potential," is the first and original man, and every people that has color came from black people—which include brown people, red people, and yellow people. However, white people could not come from black people because white is the absence of color and color only produces color, just as you can't get color from non-color.

The German professor Arnold Ehret, in his book *Mucusless Diet and Healing System,* stated that "the white race is an unnatural, a sick, a pathological one. First, the colored skin pigment is lacking, due to a lack of coloring mineral salts; second, the blood is continually over-filled by white blood corpuscles, mucus, waste with white color—therefore, the white appearance of the entire body . . . No wonder that he looks white and pale and anaemic. Everybody knows that an extreme case of paleness is a 'bad sign.' . . . Civilized men of our race show by their white skin that they are sick from birth on; they inherit the mucused, white blood corpuscles—the 'sign of death.' " Understand that this is from a European professor—but not only European, a German European whose race has always preached the purity and superiority of the Aryan people.

When Johari Amini stated, in *An Afrikan Frame of Reference,* published by the Institute of Positive Education, that "a working definition is a determinant of behavior," she is saying that a person's "patterns of behavior" that develop over a period of time are very complex, yet, logical and systematic. Our entire *definition process*— that is, how we define, interpret, perceive, and function has been operating from an "anti-frame of reference." Our definitions have been molded in an anti-black, anti-Afrikan frame of reference which is an "anti-frame of reference" for us; they are not legitimate for our use and will, by definition, work against us. In order for them to function for us, they must be re-defined from an Afrikan Frame of Reference.

Dr. Welsing's Theory of Color-Confrontation states that "the white or color deficient Europeans responded psychologically with a profound sense of numerical inadequacy and color inferiority upon their confrontations with the massive majority of the world's people, all of whom possessed varying degrees of color-producing capacity. This psychological response, be it described as conscious or unconscious, was one of deeply sensed inadequacy which struck a blow at the most obvious and fundamental part of their being, their external appearance."

If we keep in mind what Johari Amini has said about frame of reference and definitions, and what Dr. Welsing has said about the inadequacy of Europeans in terms of color and numbers, you can begin to see the direction in which I'm going—in order for the Europeans to compete and control the world on terms that are beneficial to them, they had to develop a *frame of reference* which would, in essence, turn the definitions of the world around. Dr. Welsing states that psychologically, the Europeans began to exhibit "an uncontrollable sense of hostility and aggression developed defensively, which has continued to manifest itself throughout the entire historical epoch of the mass confrontations of the whites with people of color." And have been directed toward the Blacks, "non-white" people who have the greatest color potential, and therefore, are the most envied and the most feared in genetic color competition.

Due to their "numerical inadequacy and genetic color inferiority" the Europeans developed a number of "psychological defensive maneuvers or defensive mechanisms." Dr. Welsing says that the "initial psychological defense maneuver was the 'repression' of the initial void—being without color and numerical in the minority—both were hard to take and adjust to, so both were repressed and defensive mechanisms built to protect their sense of inadequacy and incompleteness. Dr. Welsing also observed in their behavior pattern a phenonmenon she describes as the "reaction formation," another mechanism produced by Europeans as a response to their situation. The "reaction formation" was (at the psychological level) to convert anything that was "desired and envied (skin color) but which was wholly unattainable" by Europeans into the "undesired," and is to be "discredited and despised." The Europeans, "desiring to have skin color, but being unable to achieve this end on their own, said, in effect, consciously or unconsciously, that skin color was degrading to them and began attributing negative qualities to color, and especially to the state of most skin color—Blackness." Thus, for us started what Johari Amini calls our Anti-Frame of Reference, but for the Europeans, was the initiation of a European or white frame of reference, which would curse the Afrikan, Asian, and Indian world. The anti-frame of reference is being made by someone who has white skin and "whose value system has determined that this is a credible standard of beauty. This frame of reference can be called an anti-frame of reference for us, if we do not see standards of beauty in terms of ourselves, from the View Points of Us, but instead, accept someone else's definitions as our own." This anti-frame of reference, forced on the "non-white" people of the world through the raw and uninhibited use of power, religion, technology, science, and "advanced" social myths, is about the major obstacle we face today as a people.

To function under someone else's frame of reference is not only dangerous but destructive—we, by definition, adapt to their self-image, to their self-concept. And even though it is destructive to us, it is constructive for the European. The frame of reference under which we operate, by definition, is dangerous to us and by definition, if it is dangerous to us it must be beneficial to our enemies.

Briefly what we've tried to tell you is that: one, we must stop reacting to white and start acting for ourselves; two, we must consciously and unconsciously reorder the definitions of the world into their rightful frames of reference in order to function at all times in the best interest of Afrikan People; and three, we Black people must begin to understand that white people, "being acutely aware of their lack of or inferior genetic ability to produce skin color, built the elaborate myth of white genetic superiority. They then set about the long drawn-out task of evolving a social, political, and economic structure with all attendant institutions, to give Blacks and other "non-whites" the appearance of being inferior human beings."*

Their genetic and numerical inadequacy can be linked to most of the evil in the world today. They cannot produce color, thus, they hate color and by hating color, again, they hate their lack of color. Out of this comes the whole gamut of sexual myths and distortions, come the religious and world philosophies that categorized blacks as evil and played down sex as uncivilized. It is commonly known today that "if hate and lack of respect are outwardly manifested toward others, hate and lack of respect are most often found at deeper levels toward the self." Yet, to preserve the self-entity is to degrade everybody else. In the European-American frame of reference, people of color become the minorities, and are, in reality, the majorities, and all kinds of tricks are tried to keep us apart and fighting among ourselves.

It is time to understand that Afrikans, Asians, and Indians are in the majority, that the white "race" collectively represents the world's largest minority and will push birth control, population control, and anything else on us to stop the reproductive process. The white "race," in terms of its own frame of reference, always presents itself

---

*Dr. Welsing. *Theory of Color-Confrontation*

as the world's majority, and the "true numerical majority (the 'non-whites') illusionally feels and views itself as the minority." Their efforts to maintain control of the world by "divide and conquer" can be seen in all spectrum of the Afrikan world. Through their various agencies, they construct coups and "initiate conflict" between brothers and brothers, and brothers and neighbors. This is how a "minority" can remain in power through the "divide, Frictionalyze, and Conquer pattern," observable throughout the known universe wherever whites are confronted by "non-whites."

We ask you at this time to begin to reconstruct your own frame of reference based upon a sound black value system (we suggest the Nguzo Saba, recreated by Maulana Karenga). Only out of a new Afrikan set of directives can we begin to see the evil of the Europeans and European-Americans, and if we continue to absorb their philosophy—religious and secular—there is no way in the world that we will be able to survive as a people. Ask your grandfather about this—he may remember that:

In Afrika
in ancient times
people did not try to
be, look or live white   because
white was not a color
white was the absence of color.
all that was evil in the land was white.
all that was death in the land was white
white was not a color   it was the absence of color

in the modern times
things have not changed much   except
some people are trying to
be, look and live white   not realizing that
white is not a color
white is the absence of color
all that is evil in the world is white
all that is death in the world is white
when you see people who are white
know that they are evil and death
is not far behind.

Culture/Commitment/
Conclusions for Action

OUR INABILITY AS A PEOPLE TO THINK CRITICALLY about and question our position in this world at any given time has ruled us defenseless and powerless in a political, technological and historical world based upon defense and power. To be apolitical, atechnological and ahistorical (which by definition rules us inactive) in the Seventies is the highest compliment that can be paid to the effectiveness of the European-American educational system; it has rendered us almost completely ignorant of the world we occupy and totally dependent upon other people for *all* our lifegiving and lifesaving resources, e.g., water, food, housing, clothing, education, etc. We have, whether we admit it or not, been molded into beings that are mentally—in terms of our existence—just above *animals,* and just as animals, we are ruled by instincts which govern us from day to day; we are not aware of our lives in a political, technological, or historical context, and as a result, seldom analyze our lives in a national or international context, which means that, as Afrikan people, we have not been able to nationalize, organize, or mobilize at a local or a world level to challenge the rule of the worldrunners: European-Americans.

This essay, realistically, poses and attempts to answer only a few of the serious questions in terms of our survival. And it seems to me that our inability in the past to seriously deal with these questions at a new level is partially why we're in such a sad situation today. I believe that it was Fanon who said that "each generation must out of relative obscurity discover its mission, fulfill it, or betray it." What is the mission of the Afrikan in America—better yet —in the world? Why is it that we're only crisis-oriented? Why do we only deal with the immediate rather than prepare for the coming.

Why is it in our attempt to be different that we become so much alike? Even though we wear *their* clothes better than they do, drive *their* cars faster than they do, play *their* games better than they do, use *their* language as well as they do—it still spells out to be *theirs*. We have internalized the oppressor's values to the point where we're *him*. We have moved so far from our actual and natural Afrikan selves that we must deal with the oppressor within before we can effectively take on the one outside. Since "black" is in, is there any *real* separation between black and white? Is there a black lifestyle or a *black value system?* What rules us inactive in a world of activity? Where are our institutions? We can't possibly instutionalize our thoughts and actions without institutions. What is black manhood/womanhood? Is it a duplication of white manhood/ womanhood in blackface? We're 30 million strong in this country, the largest congregation of Afrikans outside Afrika. Why is it that other ethnic groups we out-number, in some cases five to one, have more power and influence than we? Why are we not "free?" Paulo Friere says, "The oppressed, having internalized the image of the oppressor and adopted his guideline, are fearful of freedom. Freedom would require them to eject this image and replace it with autonomy and responsibility. Freedom is acquired by conquest, not by gift. It must be pursued constantly and responsibly. Freedom is not an ideal located outside man; nor is it an idea which becomes myth. It is, rather, the indispensable condition for the quest for human completeness." What have we conquered lately?

When we speak of culture we mean the beliefs and values that a people live by and guide their lives by. These values and beliefs define a people, define the purposes and direction of a people. Culture is an integral part of man's social system and at best is the basis for the social system. Through one's culture come the definitions of why a people exist and function the way they do. Roles are defined by the use of culture, and thereby personalities are formed.

One of our many difficulties living as Afrikans in America is that we never, really, define ourselves from a pure Afrikan context. This is understandable, since our personality—our individualism—has been shaped by the culture of the West. This is to say that it is unnatural for us, as an Afrikan people, to function against our own interests, but we've been taught to do that! So, in order for us to gain the impetus for struggle that is needed, we need to re-define ourselves from an Afrikan frame of reference.

The four levels of development are: ideology, organization, communications, and resources. We suggest these ten points to aid you in personal and organizational development:

1. A black value system that is consistent with our life and death struggle. We suggest the Nguzo Saba.

2. Committed black people—knowledgeable of positives and negatives of struggle and life.

3. Realistic programs that meet the needs of the people and serve the people—incorporating the Pan-Afrikan concepts of work, study, creativity, and building.

4. Realistic educational instituitons that inform, educate and listen to the people, teaching the seven principles.

5. A financial base that is within the community. If the community doesn't support it after a reasonable length of time, question your legitimacy.

6. Accountability and credibility with your people. You will not survive if European-Americans are running in and out of your operation.

7. Noticable production and results: always produce, whether goods and services or educationally.

8. Avoid contradictions: be what you teach.

9. The willingness to grow and add new blood: admit mistakes and learn from them.

10. Create an atmosphere of security and love and exemplify that in everything that you do.

145

Remember, as long as there is an enemy there will be competition. However, in our house there will be cooperation and complementary actions. We must re-create an Afrikan way of life.

It took the current leaders in China and the Chinese people 23 years to re-create a Chinese mind that is consistent and totally Chinese. The Honorable Sekou Toure, for the last ten years, in Guinea has been about the business of re-creating an Afrikan mind in Guinea, West Afrika. Yet, black people in the United States think that they can read a few books, attend a few classes, engage in a few "black" rap sessions and come out blacker than night. In part, they are right—because they're still shouting in the dark. We cannot re-create an Afrikan mind in a predominantly European setting by just reading books, attending a few classes, and engaging in dialectical discussions.

To recreate an Afrikan mind is to create an Afrikan lifestyle that is consistent and compatable with the life and death struggle we're engaged in daily—is to create in this country, sometimes under the most contradictory of circumstances, a consistency among Afrikan people that will allow us to think, act, create, and build in the best interests of the Afrikan world, while concentrating our efforts on the national local areas of struggle wherever we are.

We need a new level of commitment. This commitment to the Afrikan struggle is not an eight-hour day, 5-days a week struggle with paid vacations. I wonder how many vacations were taken when I T & T was being built—how many coffee breaks were allowed when Ford was being built—how many days off for false sickness were allowed with GM? The Vietnamese people are not sun bathing in the Bahamas; the brothers and sisters in Guinea Bissau take few coffee breaks; yet, the insecure blood here always asks "When is the revolution coming?", not realizing that we're already in it; not realizing that there are phases to revolution, he seeks a projected date and asks, "Will it be next week? Six months from now, or by Christmas?" We should answer him by saying that if he's still celebrating Christmas, the revolution may never come for him; on the other hand, if he had his eye on reality he would have realized that we're in the worst of the struggle now—the revolution to win the minds of our people. This is important because it seems that every twenty years we discover that we're black, as if blackness was something new, and that our generation, out of its foresight and special knowledge, invented it.

Where are our committed *men?* We're all committed to do something—some of us to our cars, some to women, some to the white boy or girl. Most of us view commitment as being defined by the person making it—that is, if the organization has no sayso over your time, your time will remain your own, coming and going as you please in your own context. Commitment is *not* when you can find time to fit yourself in, but is how the organization can best use your talents while keeping an eye on reality and the practical and potential application of your time.

That is, we know you have to work, but you don't tell the white boy that you can't make it—you're on the job every day because it's important to your survival. The nationalist organization, if defined properly, is more important than that job because it's concerned about you. Theoretically, there are levels of commitment depending on one's consciousness. But, one would have to doubt one's commitment if the blood is living in a $65,000 home and driving all kinds of big cars while dressing like a castrated European. The new commitment deals with what we call Ujamaa (Cooperative Economics) and Ujima (Collective Work and Responsibility). We feel that it is a crime against our children and our ancestors to see some of our people living like they're in another world. The realworld in! The New Commitment means that you not only commit your time and effort, but all your resources to the organization that is genuinely working for us. You shouldn't have a large bank account stashed away, or secret investments in stocks and bonds—all that says is that you're not really concerned about struggle, because in the final comedown, the big house, new cars, stylish clothes, bank accounts, and financial investments are investments in this country, and people only invest in something they believe in. People who invest at that level in this country really don't want to see a change —because that change will effect them too.

We can also look at commitment in terms of the family structure. Your house must be in order. You and your woman must be going in the same direction. We lose too many brothers and sisters who are committed to the struggle—but in different ways. Or, one may be committed and the other is not, which is just as bad, because one-half of a household is no house. The brother should be strong enough to bring his sister into the struggle—if he's not, *we must question him.* There is a basic contradiction in his family life if he's dedicated and she's not, or vice-versa. The "house is the smallest unit of the nation" and if it's not together, the nation is not together.

Finally, we must understand that the Europeans are committed to maintaining their control over the world. It should be obvious to us by now that they're playing for keeps. In their madness, if the choice were to lose it or destroy it, destruction would be forthcoming. I say this again, to emphasize the enemy we're dealing with. Power is the determinant. In this country it doesn't matter what you do as long as you have the power to back it up; and, if you are sophisticated, you'll say it's in the name of Jesus Christ or democracy. Define yourself and you define the enemy.

> We
> as sane men
> would like to see that
> black and white and red and yellow and brown men
> live together in
> peace and harmony   yet
> white men
> will not allow the *world* to live in
> peace and harmony   and
> we
> as sane men
> must fight.
>
>   Asante Sana

Worldview:
Toward a Functional Reading List

THIS BOOK LIST IS TO SERVE SEVERAL FUNCTIONS: AS a reading and reference list for a number of courses I'm teaching—specifically, *Worldview: Toward a New Consciousness*—and as a guide to other resources. In my travels, many brothers and sisters have asked me about the books that have influenced me the most. That in itself is almost an impossible question to answer, especially, if books are a part of one's lifestyle. This is to say that I have been influenced by many books and I undoubtedly left out some very important titles. However, this list is not to be all inclusive (it was not meant to be); it is only to serve as a guide to your own list. I must also add that books are fine if used properly, that is, to serve as educating vehicles to stimulate one to take an active part in this world. I have very little respect for the "scholar" who does nothing but read, research, and write. To understand our life and death struggle and not be actively involved in that struggle at a black organizational and black institutional level, to me, is a *crime*. The world is not only controlled by men with "knowledge" but by men who mis-use "knowledge" and to possess "knowledge" and not use it for the betterment of Afrikan people is, in my value system, a mis-use.

AFRIKA,
PAN-AFRIKANISM, COLONIALISM:

Aime Cesaire. *Discourse on Colonialism.*
Albert Memmi. *The Colonized and the Colonizer.*
Albert Memmi. *Dominated Man.*
Frantz Fanon. *The Wretched of the Earth.*
Frantz Fanon. *Black Skins/White Masks.*
Kwame Nkrumah. *Neo-Colonialism: The Last Stage of Imperialism.*
Kwame Nkrumah. *Dark Days in Ghana.*
George Padmore. *How Britain Rules Africa.*
Jack Woodis. *Introduction to Neocolonialism.*
Waldemar A. Nielsen. *The Great Powers and Africa.*
Raymond F. Betts, ed. *The "Scramble" For Africa.*
Oginga Odinga. *Not Yet Uhuru.*
Leonard Barnes. *African Renaissance.*
Leonard Barnes. *Africa in Eclipse.*

HISTORY AND ANALYSIS
OF AFRIKAN HISTORICAL MOVEMENTS:

V. B. Thompson. *Africa and Unity.*
George Padmore. *History of the Pan African Movement.*
George Padmore. *Pan Africanism or Communism.*
The Center for Black Education. *African Liberation.*
Chancellor Williams. *Rebirth of African Civilization.*
Chancellor Williams. *The Destruction of Black Civilization.*
Ali A. Mazrui. *Toward A Pax Africana.*
C. L. R. James. *A History of Pan African Revolt.*
Yosef ben Jochannon. *Black Man of the Nile.*
Yosef ben Jochannon. *Africa: Mother of "Western Civilization."*
W. E. B. DuBois. *The World and Africa.*
Wilfred Cartey and Martin Kilson. *The African Reader: Independent and Colonial,* (Volumes 1 and 2).
John G. Jackson. *Introduction to African Civilization.*

AFRIKAN STRUGGLE
AND NATIONALISM:

Amilcar Cabral. *Armed Struggle in Africa.*
Amilcar Cabral. *Revolution in Guinea.*
Ndabanings Sithole. *African Nationalism.*
Kwame Nkrumah. *Africa Must Unite.*

Kwame Nkrumah. *I Speak of Freedom.*
Kwame Nkrumah. *Challenge of the Congo.*
Aime Cesaire. *A Season in the Congo.*
Patrice Lumumba. *My Last Days in the Congo.*
Shawna Maglanbayan. *Garvey, Lumumba, Malcolm: Black Nationalist Separatists.*
J. M. Kariuki. *Mau Mau Detainee.*
Frantz Fanon. *Studies in a Dying Colonialism.*
Robert F. Williams. *Negroes With Guns.*
E. Essien-Udom. *Black Nationalism.*
Kwame Nkrumah. *Handbook of Revolutionary Warfare.*
Leiden and Schmidt. *The Politics of Assassination.*
William Pomeroy. *Guerilla Warfare and Marxism.*
Eduardo Mondalane. *Armed Struggle in Mozambique.*
Patrice Lumumba. *Congo My Country.*
Amy Jacques Garvey. *Garvey and Garveyism.*
Sami Hadawi. *Bitter Harvest* (Palestine 1914-67).
Walter Rodney. *How Europe Underdeveloped Africa.*
Don L. Lee. *Europe and Afrika: A Poet's View—Part 1.*

RELIGIONS AND PHILOSOPHY:

Yosef ben-Jochannon. *African Origins of the Major "Western Religions."*
St. Clair Drake. *Redemption of Africa and Black Religion.*
John S. Mbiti. *African Religion and Philosophies.*
Cheikh Anta Diop. *The Culture Unity of Negro Africa.*
Edward Blyden. *Christianity, Islam and the Negro Race.*
The Holy Bible.
The Holy Koran.
Lao Tzu. *The Way of Life.*
E. A. Wallis Budge. *The Egyptian Book of the Dead.*
Kahlil Gibran. *The Prophet.*
Bertrand Russell. *Why I Am Not a Christian.*
Maryam Jameelah. *Islam and Modernism.*
The Upanishads: *Breath of the Eternal.* Translated by Prabhavananda & Manchester.
The Living Talmud. Translated by Judah Goldin.
The I Ching or Book of Changes. Translated by Wilhelm & Baynes.
The Song of God: Bhagavad-Gita. Translated by Prabhavananda & Isherwood.
The Sayings of Confusius. Translated by James R. Ware.

Elijah Muhammad. *Message to the Black Man.*
Jack Mendelsohm. *God, Allah and Juju.*
Lao Tzu (interpreted by Archie Bohm.) *Tao Teh King.*
Maulana Karenga. *The Quotable Karenga.*
Maulana Karenga. *Kitabu: Beginning Concepts in Kawaida.*

WORLD POLITICS AND STRUGGLE:

Elie Kedourie. *Nationalism in Asia and Africa.*
Brian Crozier. *The Masters of Power.*
Brian Crozier. *The Morning After.*
Pierre Jalee. *The Pillage of the Third World.*
Pierre Jalee. *The Third World in World Economy.*
Pierre Jalee. *Imperialism in the Seventies.*
Rupert Emerson. *From Empire to Nation.*
George W. Shepherd, Ed. *Racial Influence in American Foreign Policy.*
Albert K. Weinberg. *Manifest Destiny.*
Leonard Slater. *The Pledge: Eye of the Enemy.*
Samuel Yette. *The Choice.*
Boyd C. Shafer. *Nationalism, Myth and Reality.*
Paulo Friere. *Pedagogy of the Oppressed.*
Herman Kahn. *On Thermonuclear War.*
Herman Kahn. *Thinking about the Unthinkable.*
Herman Kahn. *On Escalation.*
Leonard C. Lewin, ed. *Report from Iron Mountain.*
Hans Kohn. *The Idea of Nationalism.*
Stokely Carmichael. *Stokely Speaks.*

ASIA:

Frantz Schurmann. *Ideology and Organization in Communist China.*
Mao Tse-Tung. *The Selected Works of Mao Tse-Tung.* Edited by Shaw, Bruno.
Ross Terril, 800,000,000, *The Real China.*
Alan P. L. Liu. *Communications and National Integration in Communist China.*
Dick Wilson. *The Long March.*
Stuart Schram. *Mao Tse-Tung.*
Schurmann & Schell. *Republican China.*
Maria Antonietta Macciocchi. *Daily Life in Revolutionary China.*
Isaiah Ben-Dasan. *The Japanese and the Jews.*
Suntzu. *The Art of War.*

GOVERNMENT:

Julius Nyerere. *Freedom and Unity.*
Julius Nyerere. *Ujamaa.*
Leopold Sedar Senghor. *Nationhood and the African Road to Socialism.*
Machiavelli. *The Prince.*
C. Wright Mills. *The Power Elite.*
G. William Domhoff. *The Higher Circles.*
Person & Anderson. *The Case Against Congress.*
Green, Fallows, Zwick. *Who Runs Congress?*
Michael Harrington. *Socialism.*
Leonard C. Lewin, Ed. *The Report from Iron Mountain.*
Selected Works from Mao Tse-Tung.
Selected Works of Marx and Engels.
Robert N. Winter-Berger. *The Washington Pay Off.*
J. H. Proctor, ed. *Building Ujamaa Villages in Tanzania.* (University of Dar Es Salaam, Studies in Political Science, No. 2).
Correlli Barnett. *The Collapse of British Power.*
Correlli Barnett. *Britain and Her Army 1509-1970.*

ECONOMICS:

Cohen & Mintz. *America, Inc.*
Robert L. Allen. *Blacke Awakening in Capitalist America.*
Earl Ofari. *The Myth of Black Capitalism.*
William F. Rickenbacker. *Death of the Dollar.*
Gunnar Myrdal. *Economic Theory and Underdeveloped Regions.*
U. S. News and World Report. *Investments, Insurance, Wills, Simplified.*
Ferdinand Lunberg. *The Rich and the Super Rich.*
William Hoffman. *David: The Story of a Rockefeller.*
Richard Ney. *The Wall Street Jungle.*
Joseph C. Goulden. *The Money Givers.*
Selected Works of Mao Tse-Tung.
Selected Works of Marx and Engels.
Michael Tanzer. *Sick Society.*

NUTRITION, FOODS,
BIOLOGY AND BODY FUNCTIONS:

Jethro Kloss. *Back to Eden.*
Gordon R. Taylor. *The Biological Time Bomb.*
Herbert M. Shelton. *Health for the Millions.*
Richard Lucas. *Nature's Medicine.*

Carlson Wade. *Helping Your Health with Enzymes.*
Rachel Carson. *Silent Spring.*
William Longgood. *The Poisons in Your Food.*
Arnold Ehret. *Mucusless Diet.*
Arnold Ehret. *Rational Fasting.*
Robert Rodale, Ed. *The Basic Book of Organic Gardening.*
John T. Richter. *Nature the Healer.*
N. W. Walker. *Raw Vegetable Juices.*
G. J. Binding. *Soya Beans.*
Barry Commoner. *The Closing Circle.*
Gen. Choi Hong Hi. *Tae Kwon-Do.*
A. Westbrook and O. Ratti. *Alkido and the Dynamic Sphere.*
Johari M. Amini. *Common-Sense Approach to Eating.*

FOREIGN AFFAIRS:

Robert A. Divine, ed. *America's Foreign Policy Since 1945.*
Ronald Steel. *Pax Americana.*
Ronald Steel. *Imperialists and Other Heroes.*
Ronald Segal. *Race War.*
Ronald Segal. *The Americans: A Conflict of Greed and Reality.*
John F. Campbell. *The Foreign Affairs Fudge Factory.*
William G. Carleton. *The Revolution in American Foreign Policy.*
Henry Kissinger. *American Foreign Policy.*
Rudolf Von Albertini. *De-Colonization: The Administration and Future of the Colonies, 1919-1960.*
Herman Kahn. *The Emerging Japanese Superstate: Challenge and Response.*
George Thayer. *The War Business.*
Gabriel Kolko. *The Roots of American Foreign Policy.*
Joyce and Gabriel Kolko. *The Limits of Power.*
Richard Barnet. *Intervention and Revolution.*
J. Bowyer Bell. *The Myth of the Guerilla.*
Michael T. Klare. *War Without End.*
Frances Fitzgerald. *Fire in the Lake.*
F. S. Northedge & M. J. Grieve. *A Hundred Years of International Relations.*

PSYCHOLOGY, SOCIOLOGY, EDUCATION AND POLITICS:

Sidney M. Wilhelm. *Who Needs the Negro?*
Paul Dickson. *Think Tanks.*

B. F. Skinner. *Beyond Freedom and Dignity.*
Samuel Yette. *The Choice.*
The Center for Black Education. *The Struggle for Black Education.*
Lerone Bennett, Jr. *The Challenge of Blackness.*
George Jackson. *Soledad Brother.*
George Jackson. *Blood in My Eye.*
Imamu Amiri Baraka. *The New Nationalist.*
Imamu Amiri Baraka. *Home.*
Imamu Amiri Baraka, ed. *African Congress: A Documentary of the First Modern Pan African Congress.*
Frank Goble. *The Third Force.*
Meyer Kahane. *Never Again!*
Sterling D. Plumpp. *Black Rituals.*
Hoyt W. Fuller. *Journey to Africa.*
Bracey, Meier, Rudwick. *Black Nationalism in America.*
Harold Cruse. *The Crisis of the Negro Intellectual.*
Shawna Maglanbayan. *Garvey, Lumumba, Malcolm: Black Nationalist Separatists.*
E. Franklin Frazier. *Black Bourqeoise.*
Viktor E. Franki. *Man's Search for Meaning.*
Richard Wright. *White Man, Listen!*
W. E. B. DuBois. *Black Reconstruction.*
St. Clair Drake and Horace Cayton. *Black Metropolis.*
Richard Wright. *Black Power.*
Nathan Hare. *The Black Anglo Saxons.*
Marshall McLuhan. *Understanding Media.*
Carter G. Woodson. *Mis-education of the Negro.*
Oliver C. Cox. *Caste, Class and Race.*
Truman Nelson. *The Torture of Mothers.*
Ivan Illich. *Deschooling Society.*
Eric Fromm. *The Forgotten Language.*
Walter Lippmann. *Public Opinion.*
J. W. Fulbright. *The Pentagon Propaganda Machine.*
Dee Brown. *Bury My Heart at Wounded Knee.*
Jerome Rothenberg, Ed. *Technicians of the Sacred.*
H. Bennett. *No More Public Schools.*
Father Camilo Torres. *Revolutionary Writing.*
Herman Kahn and Briggs. *Things to Come.*
Hans Kohn. *The Idea of Nationalism.*
Leiden & Schmitt. *The Politics of Violence: Revolution in the Modern World.*
Arthur D. Morse. *While 6 Million Died.*

Vine Deloria. *We Talk You Listen.*
Vine Deloria. *Custer Died for Your Sins.*
Angela Y. Davis. *If They Come in the Morning.*
Johari M. Amini. *An African Frame of Reference.*
Hoyt W. Fuller. *The Turning of The Wheel/or Are Black Men Serious.*
Charlie Cobb. *Africa Notebook: Views on Returning "Home."*
Carlos Moore. *Were Marx and Engels White Racists?*
Lerone Bennett. *Unity in the Black Community.*
Addison Gayle, Jr. *The Politics of Revolution.*
Acklyn R. Lynch. *Blueprint for Change: Black Education.*
Mwalimu Owusu Sadaukai (Howard Fuller). *The Condition of Black People in the 1970's.*
Majib Peregrind-Brimah. *Architecture for Afrikans.*
Congress of African People. *Kwanza—The First Fruits. An African Holiday.*
Mwalimu Julius K. Nyerere. *Education for Self-Reliance.*

CULTURE: AFRIKANS IN AMERICA:

Ernest Gaines. *The Autobiography of Miss Jane Pittman.*
Andrew Billingsly. *Black Families in White America.*
Imamu Amiri Baraka. *Home.*
Imamu Amiri Baraka. *Black Music.*
Imamu Amiri Baraka. *Blues People.*
Imamu Amiri Baraka. *Black Magic Poems.*
Imamu Amiri Baraka. *Nation Time.*
Gwendolyn Brooks. *Report From Part One.*
Gwendolyn Brooks. *Riot.*
Gwendolyn Brooks. *Family Pictures.*
Gwendolyn Brooks. *The World of Gwendolyn Brooks.*
Houston A. Baker, Jr., ed. *Black Literature in America.*
Brown, Davis, and Lee, eds. *The Negro Caravan.*
Melvin B. Tolson. *Libretto for the Republic of Liberia.*
George Kent. *Blackness and the Adventure of Western Culture.*
Don L. Lee. *Directionscore: Selected and New Poems.*
Don L. Lee. *Dynamic Voices.*
Don L. Lee. *From Plan to Planet: Life-Studies—The Need for Afrikan Minds and Institutions.*
James Baldwin. *The Fire Next Time.*
James Baldwin. *Nobody Knows My Name.*
Richard Wright. *Black Boy.*
Richard Wright. *Native Son.*
The Complete Works of Carter G. Woodson.

The Autobiography of Malcolm X.
Eldridge Cleaver. *Soul on Ice.*
Julian Moreau. *The Black Commandos.*
John A. Williams. *The Man Who Cried I Am.*
W. E. B. DuBois. *The Souls of Black Folk.*
James W. Johnson. *Black Manhattan.*
Lerone Bennett, Jr. *Before the Mayflower.*
Lerone Bennett, Jr. *The Black Mood.*
Lewis and Waddy. *Black Artists on Art,* Volumes 1 and 2.
Addison Gayle, Jr. *The Black Aesthetic.*
Addison Gayle, Jr. *The Black Situation.*
Sterling D. Plumpp. *Blueprint for Developing Young People's Workshops:*
Francis Ward. *"Super Fly" A Political and Cultural Condemnation by the Kuumba Workshop.*
Chester Himes. *The Quality of Hurt.*
Sam Greenlee. *The Spook Who Sat by the Door.*
Sonia Sanchez. *Homecoming.*
Everett Hoagland. *Black Velvet.*
Dudley Randall. *More to Remember.*
Woodie King and Ron Milner, eds. *Black Drama Anthology.*
Margaret Walker. *For My People.*
Margaret Walker. *Jubilee.*
Mercer Cook and Stephen Henderson. *The Militant Black Writer.*
Harold Cruse. *The Crisis of the Negro Intellectual.*

BIOGRAPHY AND AUTOBIOGRAPHY:

Leslie Alexander Lacy. *The Rise and Fall of a Proper Negro.*
Gwendolyn Brooks. *Report From Part One.*
Richard Wright. *Black Boy.*
Charles Mingus. *Beneath the Underdog.*
William E. Smith. *We Must Run While They Walk.*
Langston Hughes. *I Wonder As I Wander.*
Langston Hughes. *The Big Sea.*
Regina Nadelson. *Who Is Angela Davis?*
A. B. Spellman. *Four Lives in the Bebop Business.* (re-issued under *Black Music*)
Mike Royko. *Boss: Richard J. Daley of Chicago.*
Ghana: *The Autobiography of Kwame Nkrumah.*
Autobiography of W. E. B. DuBois.
William Hoffman. *David: A Report on a Rockefeller.*
David Landau. *Kissinger the User of Power.*

W. A. Swanberg. *The Kingdom and the Power, Luce and His Empire.*

CARIBBEAN:

Rex M. Nettleford. *Identity, Race and Protest in Jamica.*
Rex M. Nettleford. *Mirror Mirror.*
Eric Williams. *The Negro in the Caribbean.*
Fidel Castro. *History Will Absolve Me.*
Malcolm Cross. *West Indian Social Problems.*

MAGAZINES, QUARTERLIES, NEWSPAPERS:

Black World.
Black Scholar.
Black Books Bulletin.
Black News.
Freedomways.
The Black Position.
Black Enterprise.
Black Creation.
Ebony.
Foreign Policy.
Foreign Affairs.
Commentary.
World.
Swiss Review of World Affairs.
Ramparts.
Newsweek.
Afrika Must Unite.

African Development.
African Progress.
Cricket.
The Black Collegian.
African World.
Muhammad Speaks.
Third World.
The Black Panther Paper.
Black NewArk.
The Nation.
New Republic.
Technology Review.
The Progressive.
Science and Public Affairs.
Fortune.
Sechaba.

About the Author

Haki R. Madhubuti is the publisher and editor of Third World Press, one of the largest Black publishing companies in the United States and abroad. He has been poet-in-residence at Cornell University, University of Illinois (Chicago). Howard University and Central State University. Mr. Madhubuti has published widely in magazines, quarterlies and newspapers. He is the recipient of the American Book Award in 1991 as well as numerous other awards and honors, including fellowships from the National Endowment for the Arts and the National Endowment for the Humanities. Mr. Madhubuti is a worldwide lecturer and has given readings and workshops at over 1,000 colleges, universities and community centers in Africa, Asia, South America, the Caribbean and the United States. He is one of the bestselling authors of poetry and nonfiction in the world. More than 3,000,000 of his books are currently in print. He is the author of 17 books; the latest, *Black Men: Obsolete, Single, Dangerous? The Afrikin American Family In Transition* has sold more than 100,000 copies.

Other published works are *Think Black* (1967), *Black Pride* (1968), *Don't Cry Scream* (1969), *We Walk the Way of the New World* (1970), *Directionscore: Selected and New Poems* (1971), *To Gwen, With Love edited with Francis Ward and Patricia L. Brown* (1971), *Dynamite Voices: BlackPoets of the 1960's* (1971), *Kwanzaa: A Progressive and Uplifting African American Holiday* (1972), *From Plan to Planet* (1973), *Book of Life* (1973), *A Capsule Course in Black Poetry Writing co-authored with Gwendolyn Brooks, Keorapetse Kgositsile and Dudley Randall* (1975), *Enemies: The Clash of Races* (1978), *Earthquakes and Sunrise Missions* (1984), *Killing Memory, Seeking Ancestors* (1987) and *Say That the River Turns: The Impact of Gwendolyn Brooks* (1987).

Mr. Madhubuti, director of the Institute of Positive Education has earned his MFA from the University of Iowa and is a professor of English at Chicago State University. He lives in Chicago with his wife and children.